SUPERHEROES ON A MEDICAL MISSION

MEDIKIDZ EXPLAIN ADHD

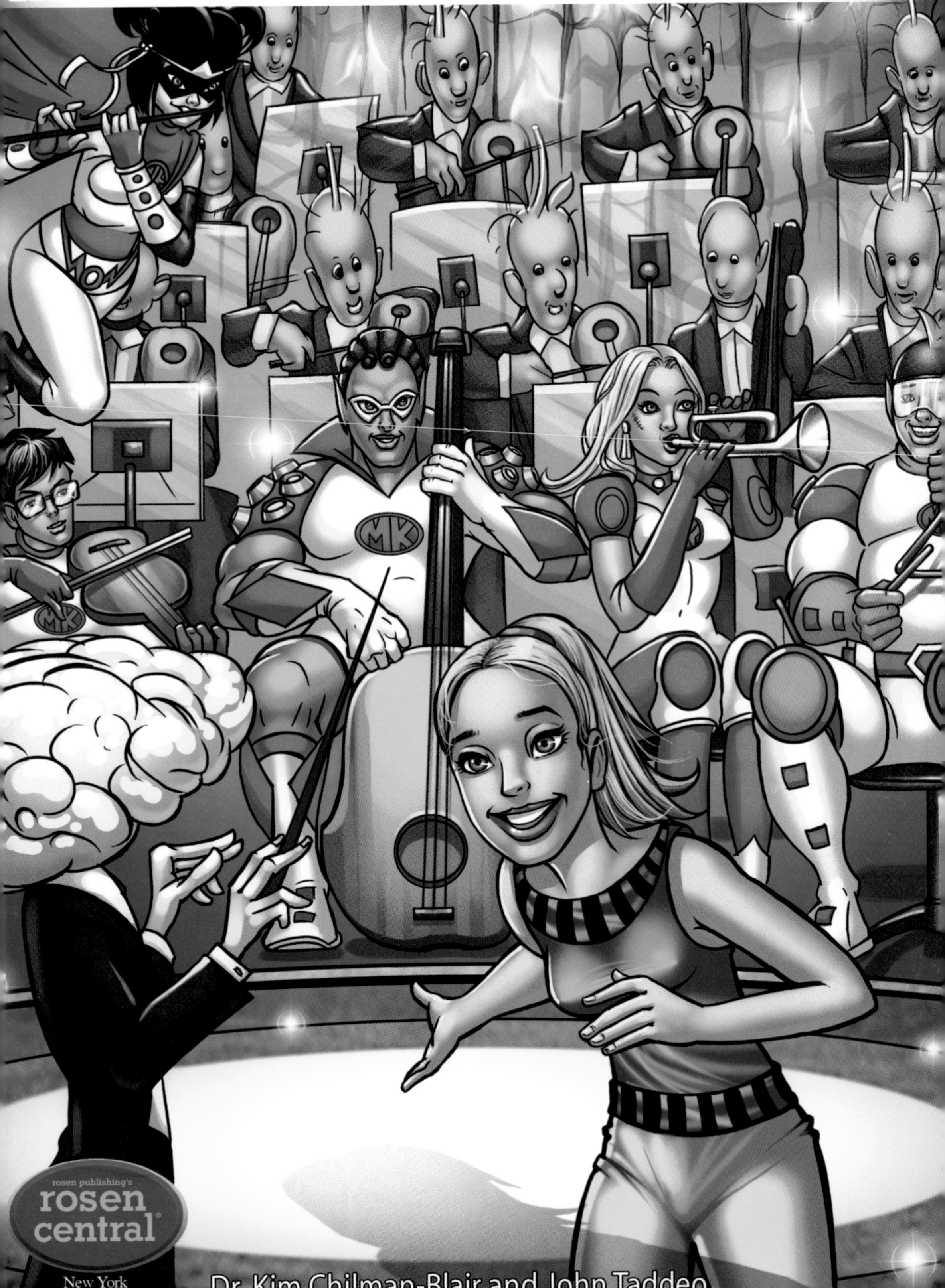

rosen publishing's
rosen central®
New York

Dr. Kim Chilman-Blair and John Taddeo
Medical content reviewed for accuracy by Professor Peter D. Hill

This edition published in 2011 by:

The Rosen Publishing Group, Inc.
29 East 21st Street
New York, NY 10010

Library of Congress Cataloging-in-Publication Data

Chilman-Blair, Kim.
Medikidz explain ADHD / Kim Chilman-Blair and John Taddeo ; medical content reviewed for accuracy by Peter D. Hill.
    p. cm. -- (Superheroes on a medical mission)
Includes index.
ISBN 978-1-4358-9456-3 (library binding) -- ISBN 978-1-4488-1833-4 (pbk.) -- ISBN 978-1-4488-1834-1 (6-pack)
1. Attention-deficit hyperactivity disorder--Comic books, strips, etc.--Juvenile literature. I. Taddeo, John. II. Title.
RJ506.H9C55 2011
618.92'8589--dc22

                                        2010001063

Manufactured in China

CPSIA Compliance Information: Batch #MS0102YA: For further information, contact Rosen Publishing, New York, New York, at 1-800-237-9932.

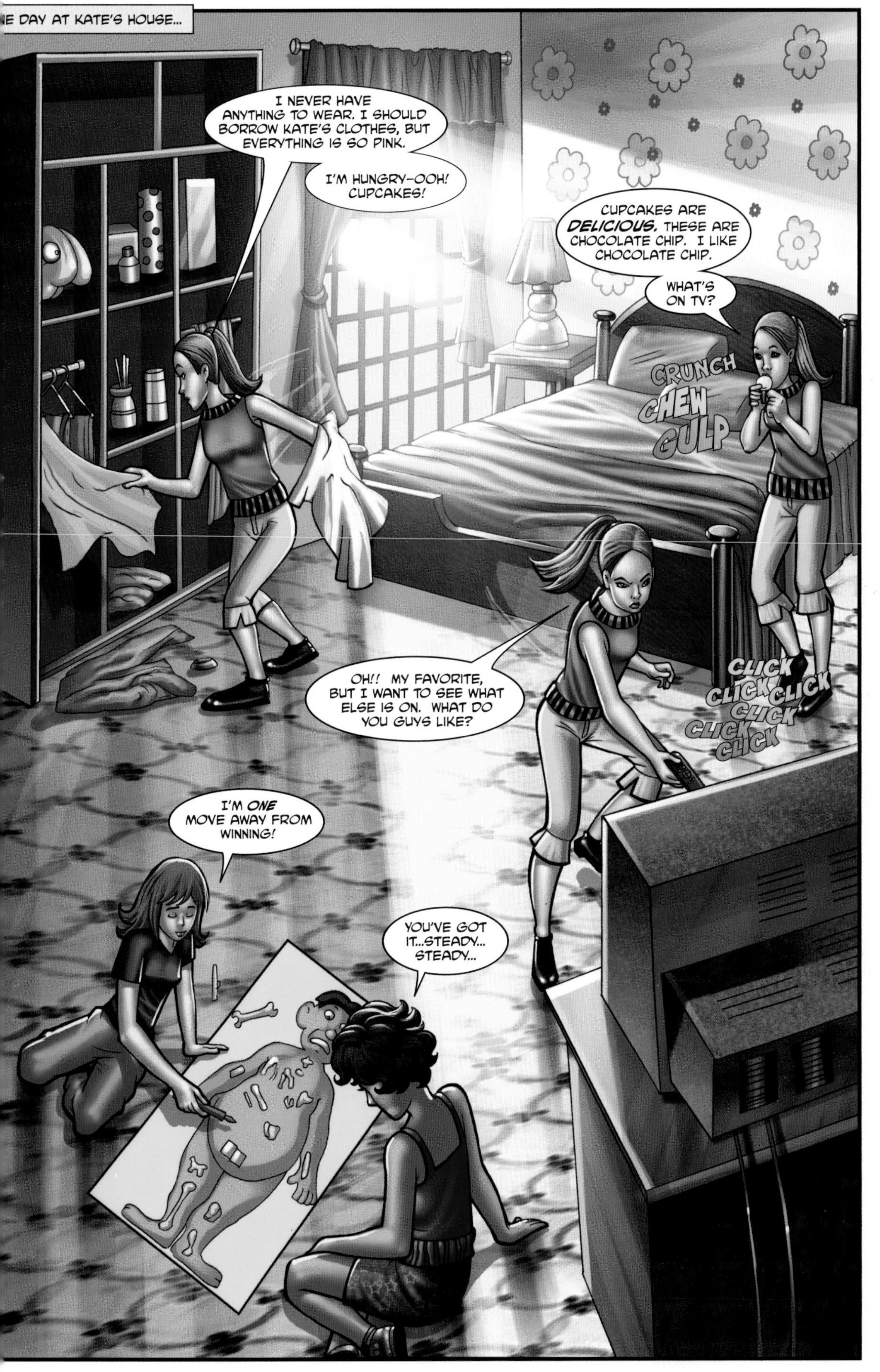
E DAY AT KATE'S HOUSE...
I NEVER HAVE ANYTHING TO WEAR. I SHOULD BORROW KATE'S CLOTHES, BUT EVERYTHING IS SO PINK.
I'M HUNGRY–OOH! CUPCAKES!
CUPCAKES ARE DELICIOUS. THESE ARE CHOCOLATE CHIP. I LIKE CHOCOLATE CHIP.
WHAT'S ON TV?
CRUNCH
CHEW
GULP
OH!! MY FAVORITE, BUT I WANT TO SEE WHAT ELSE IS ON. WHAT DO YOU GUYS LIKE?
CLICK CLICK CLICK CLICK CLICK CLICK
I'M ONE MOVE AWAY FROM WINNING!
YOU'VE GOT IT...STEADY... STEADY...

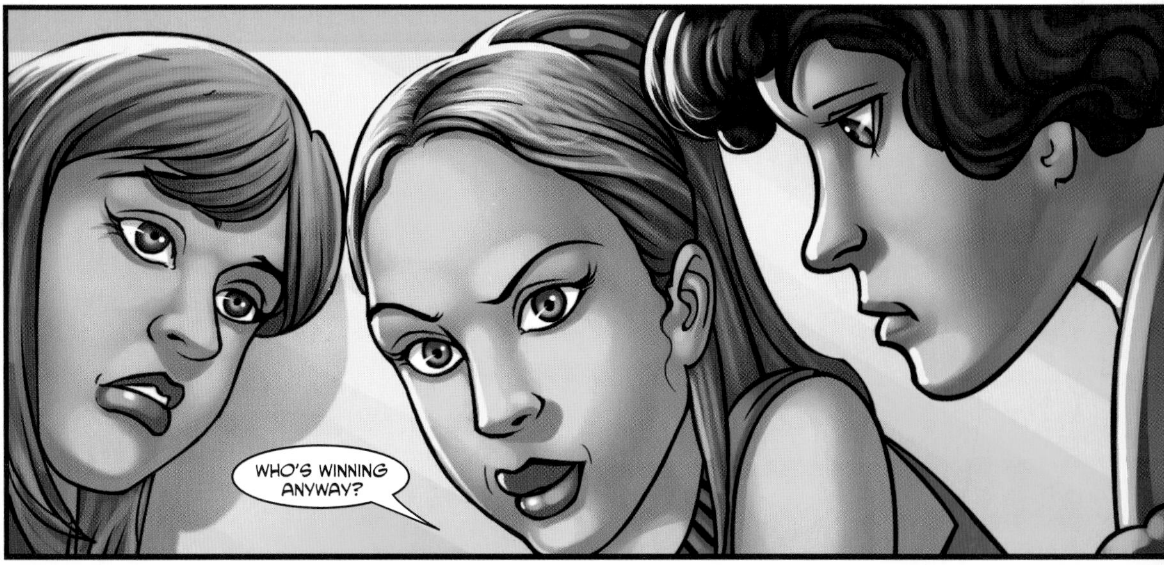
WHO'S WINNING
ANYWAY?

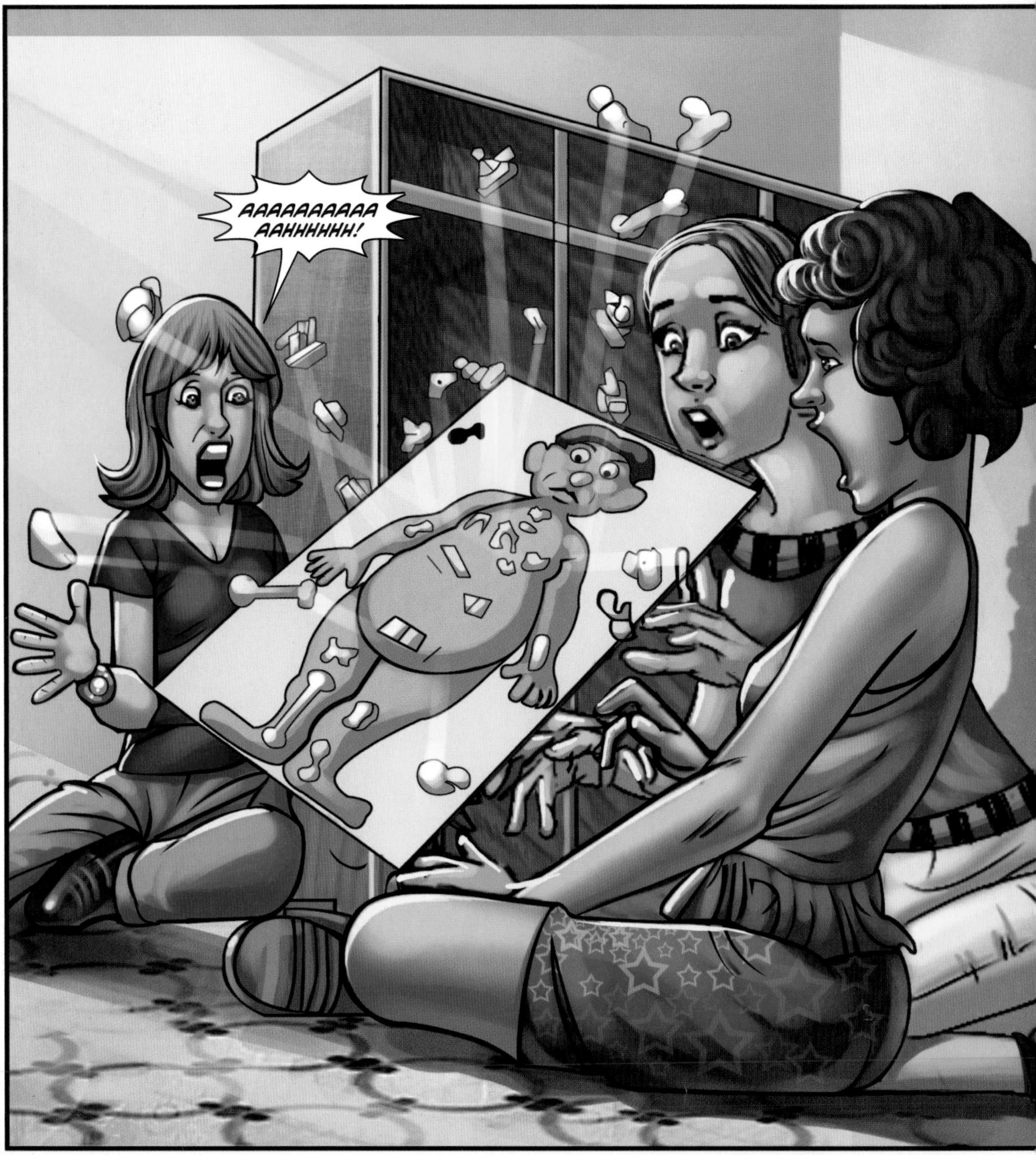
AAAAAAAAAA
AAHHHHHH!

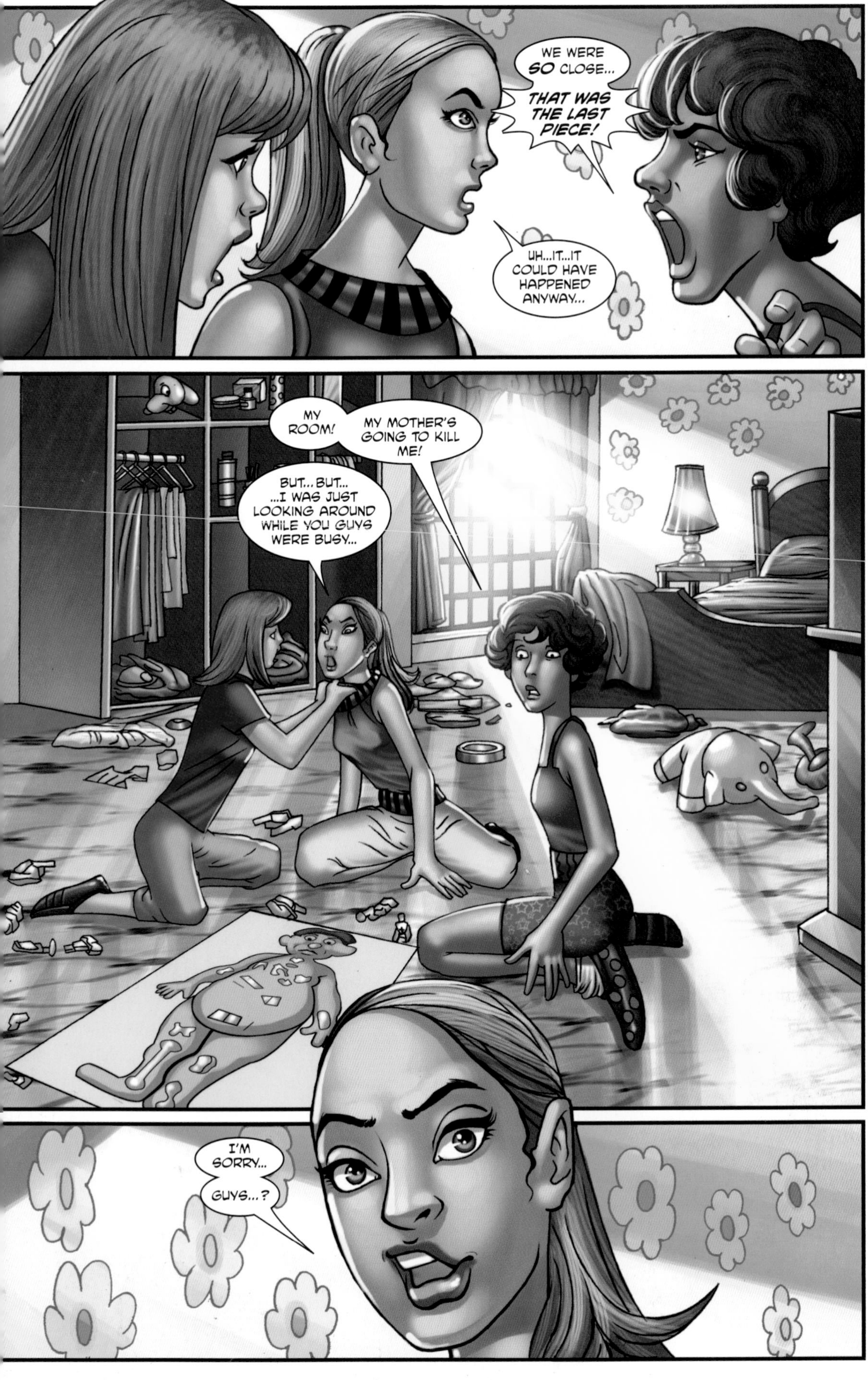
WE WERE SO CLOSE...
THAT WAS THE LAST PIECE!
UH...IT...IT COULD HAVE HAPPENED ANYWAY...
MY ROOM!
MY MOTHER'S GOING TO KILL ME!
BUT... BUT... ...I WAS JUST LOOKING AROUND WHILE YOU GUYS WERE BUSY...
I'M SORRY...
GUYS...?

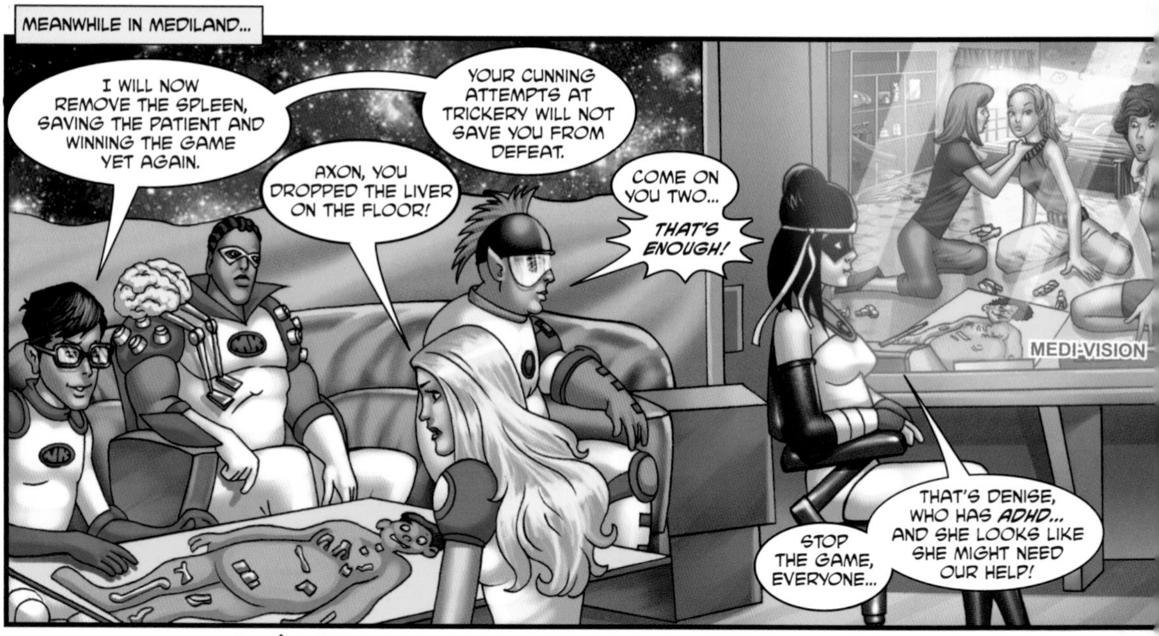
MEANWHILE IN MEDILAND...
I WILL NOW REMOVE THE SPLEEN, SAVING THE PATIENT AND WINNING THE GAME YET AGAIN.
YOUR CUNNING ATTEMPTS AT TRICKERY WILL NOT SAVE YOU FROM DEFEAT.
AXON, YOU DROPPED THE LIVER ON THE FLOOR!
COME ON YOU TWO... THAT'S ENOUGH!
MEDI-VISION
STOP THE GAME, EVERYONE...
THAT'S DENISE, WHO HAS ADHD... AND SHE LOOKS LIKE SHE MIGHT NEED OUR HELP!

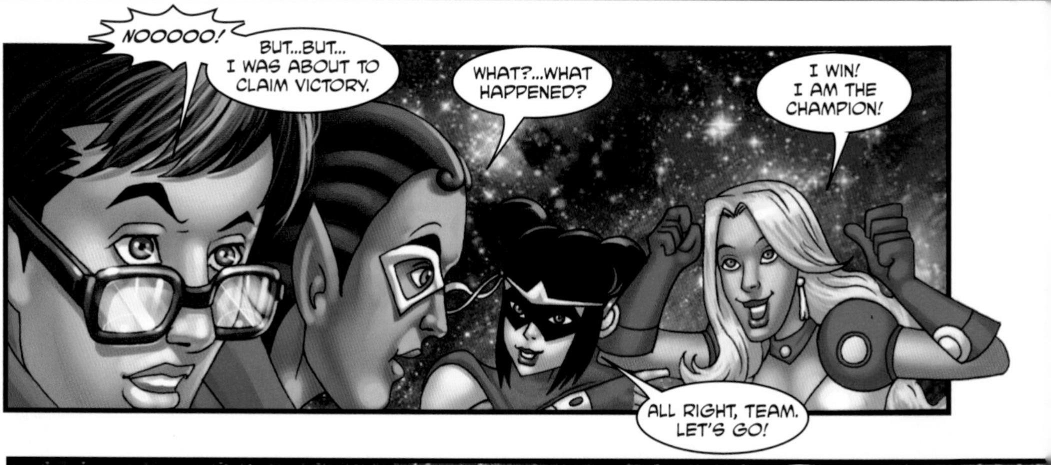
NOOOOO!
BUT...BUT... I WAS ABOUT TO CLAIM VICTORY.
WHAT?...WHAT HAPPENED?
I WIN! I AM THE CHAMPION!
ALL RIGHT, TEAM. LET'S GO!

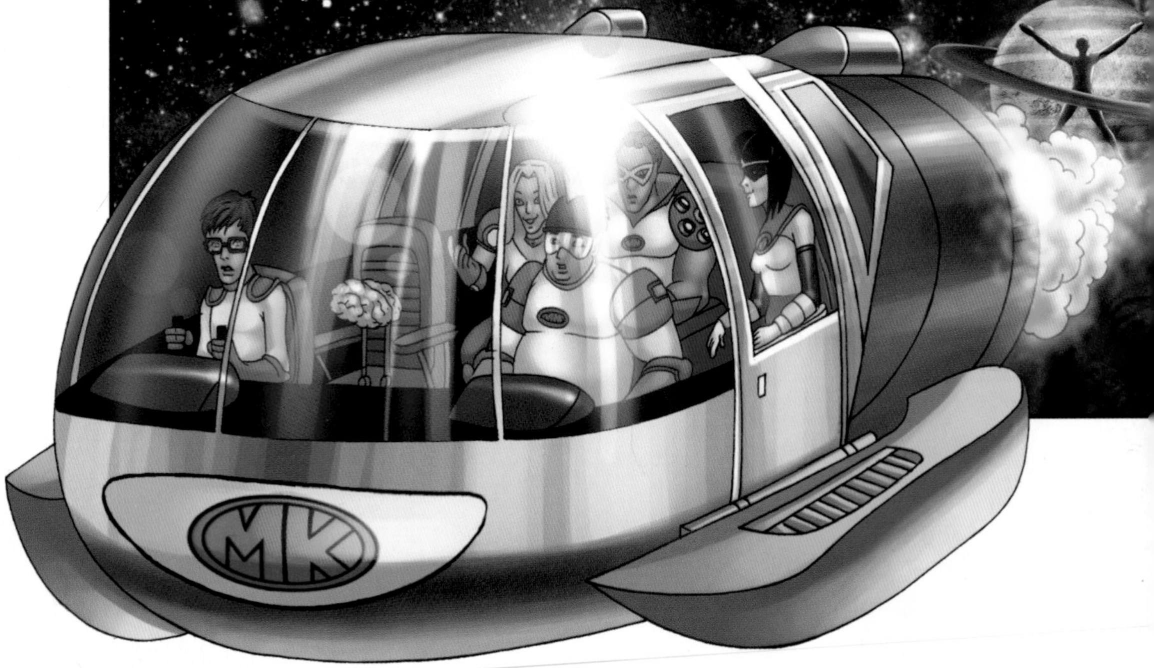
MK

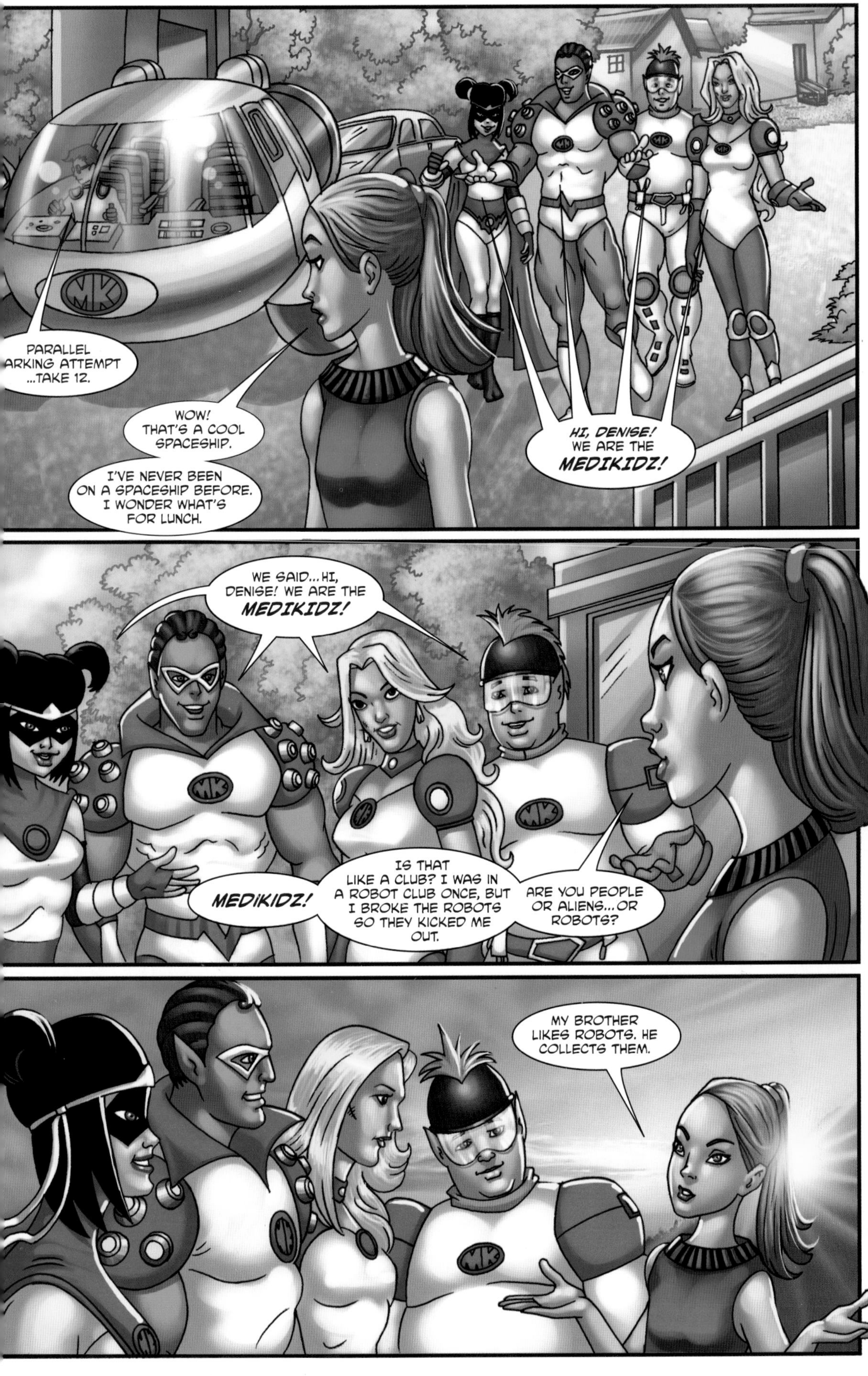
PARALLEL
ARKING ATTEMPT
...TAKE 12.
WOW!
THAT'S A COOL
SPACESHIP.
I'VE NEVER BEEN
ON A SPACESHIP BEFORE.
I WONDER WHAT'S
FOR LUNCH.
HI, DENISE!
WE ARE THE
MEDIKIDZ!
WE SAID...HI,
DENISE! WE ARE THE
MEDIKIDZ!
MEDIKIDZ!
IS THAT
LIKE A CLUB? I WAS IN
A ROBOT CLUB ONCE, BUT
I BROKE THE ROBOTS
SO THEY KICKED ME
OUT.
ARE YOU PEOPLE
OR ALIENS...OR
ROBOTS?
MY BROTHER
LIKES ROBOTS. HE
COLLECTS THEM.

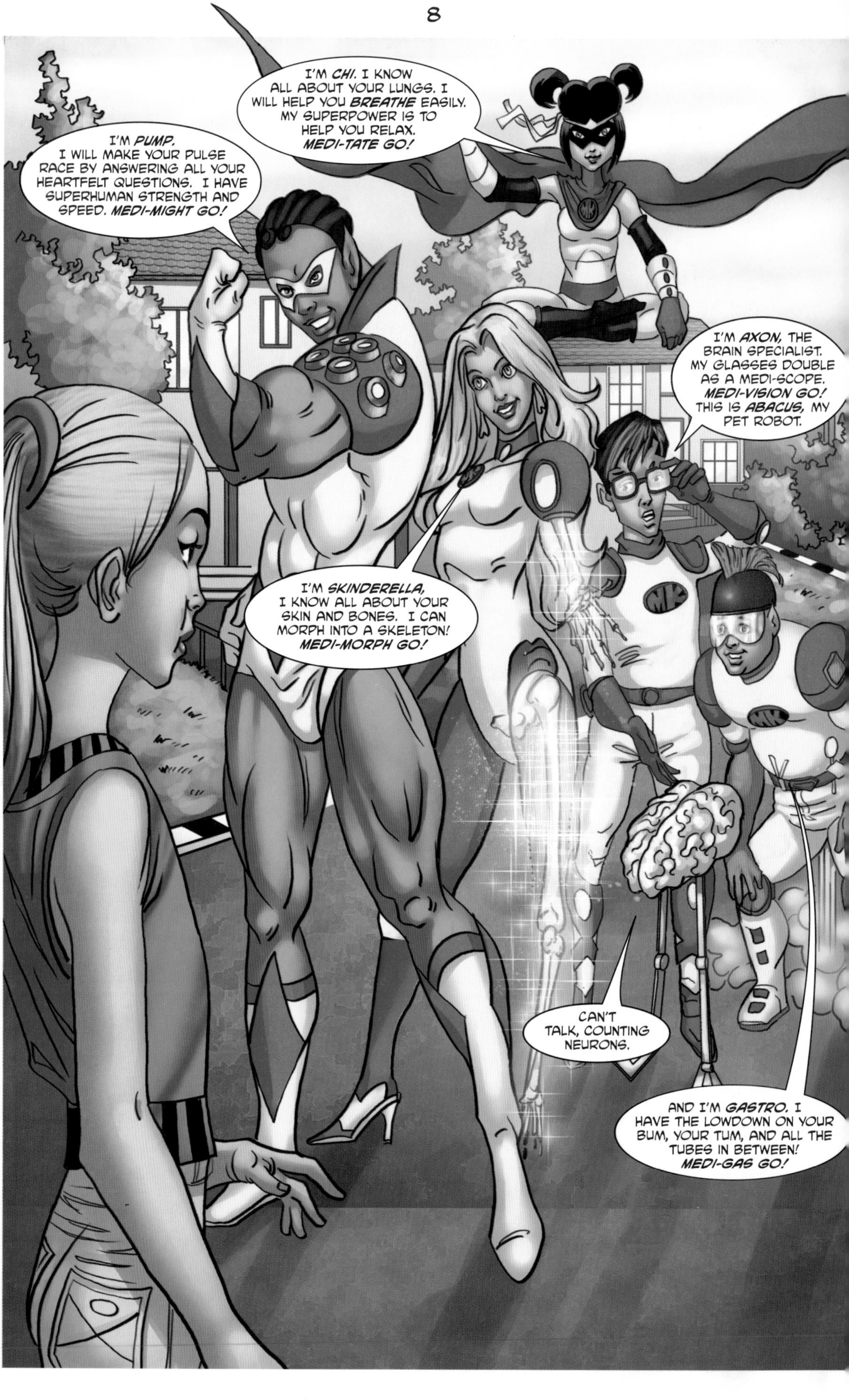
I'M PUMP.
I WILL MAKE YOUR PULSE RACE BY ANSWERING ALL YOUR HEARTFELT QUESTIONS. I HAVE SUPERHUMAN STRENGTH AND SPEED. MEDI-MIGHT GO!
I'M CHI. I KNOW ALL ABOUT YOUR LUNGS. I WILL HELP YOU BREATHE EASILY. MY SUPERPOWER IS TO HELP YOU RELAX. MEDI-TATE GO!
I'M SKINDERELLA, I KNOW ALL ABOUT YOUR SKIN AND BONES. I CAN MORPH INTO A SKELETON! MEDI-MORPH GO!
I'M AXON, THE BRAIN SPECIALIST. MY GLASSES DOUBLE AS A MEDI-SCOPE. MEDI-VISION GO! THIS IS ABACUS, MY PET ROBOT.
CAN'T TALK, COUNTING NEURONS.
AND I'M GASTRO. I HAVE THE LOWDOWN ON YOUR BUM, YOUR TUM, AND ALL THE TUBES IN BETWEEN! MEDI-GAS GO!

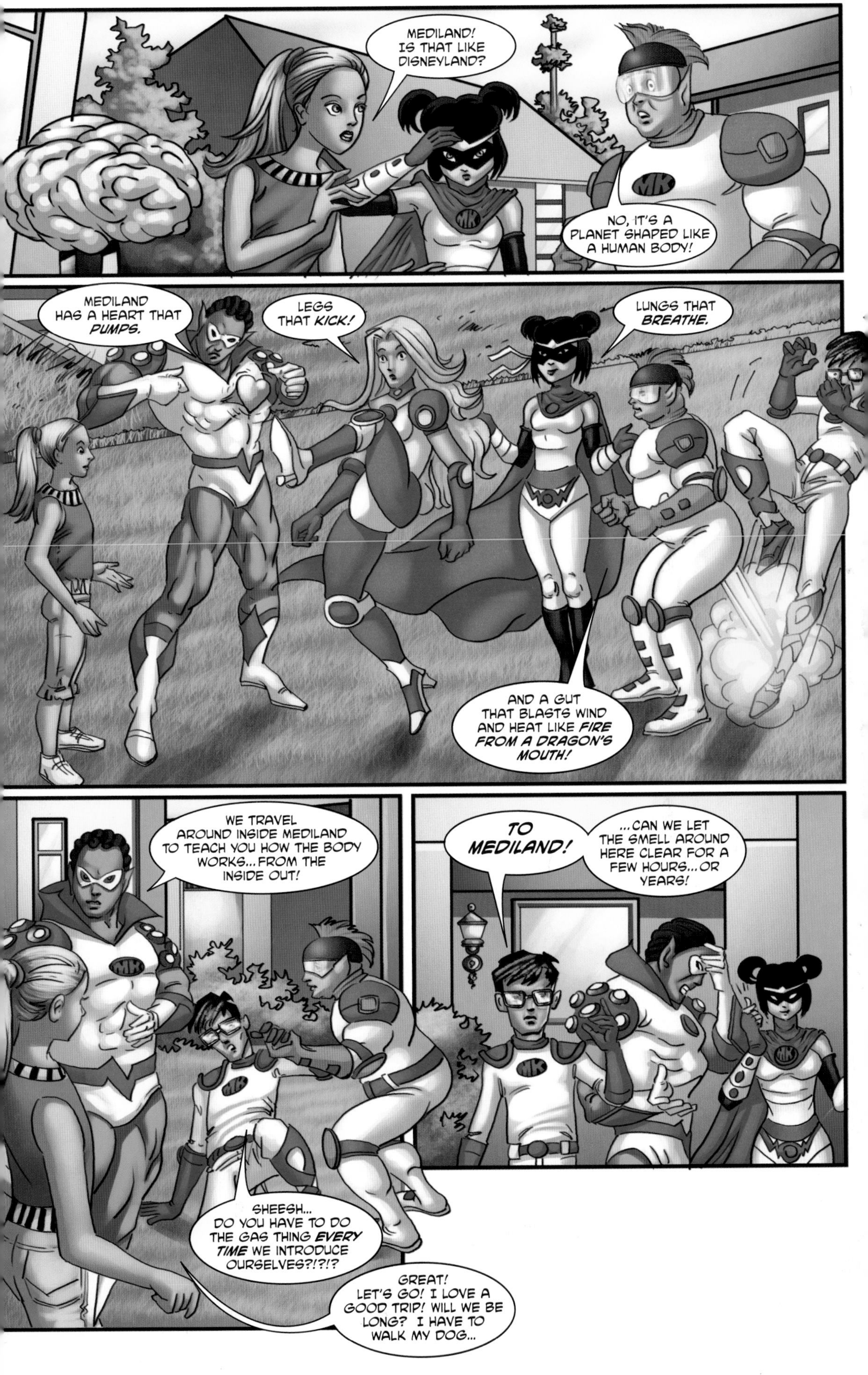
MEDILAND! IS THAT LIKE DISNEYLAND?
NO, IT'S A PLANET SHAPED LIKE A HUMAN BODY!
MEDILAND HAS A HEART THAT *PUMPS.*
LEGS THAT *KICK!*
LUNGS THAT *BREATHE.*
AND A GUT THAT BLASTS WIND AND HEAT LIKE *FIRE FROM A DRAGON'S MOUTH!*
WE TRAVEL AROUND INSIDE MEDILAND TO TEACH YOU HOW THE BODY WORKS...FROM THE INSIDE OUT!
SHEESH... DO YOU HAVE TO DO THE GAS THING *EVERY TIME* WE INTRODUCE OURSELVES?!?!?
GREAT! LET'S GO! I LOVE A GOOD TRIP! WILL WE BE LONG? I HAVE TO WALK MY DOG...
TO MEDILAND!
...CAN WE LET THE SMELL AROUND HERE CLEAR FOR A FEW HOURS...OR YEARS!

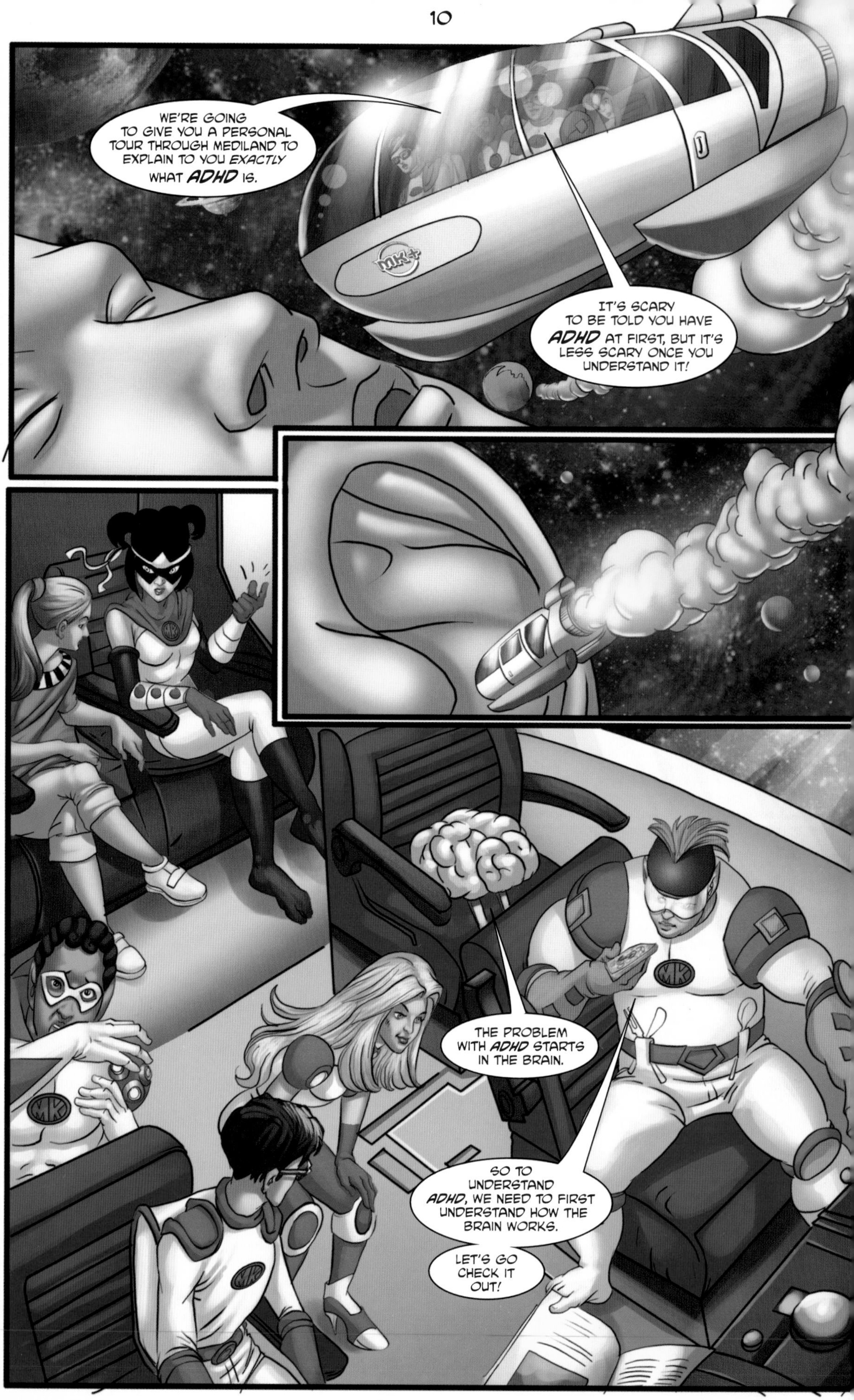
WE'RE GOING TO GIVE YOU A PERSONAL TOUR THROUGH MEDILAND TO EXPLAIN TO YOU *EXACTLY* WHAT **ADHD** IS.
IT'S SCARY TO BE TOLD YOU HAVE **ADHD** AT FIRST, BUT IT'S LESS SCARY ONCE YOU UNDERSTAND IT!
THE PROBLEM WITH **ADHD** STARTS IN THE BRAIN.
SO TO UNDERSTAND **ADHD**, WE NEED TO FIRST UNDERSTAND HOW THE BRAIN WORKS.
LET'S GO CHECK IT OUT!

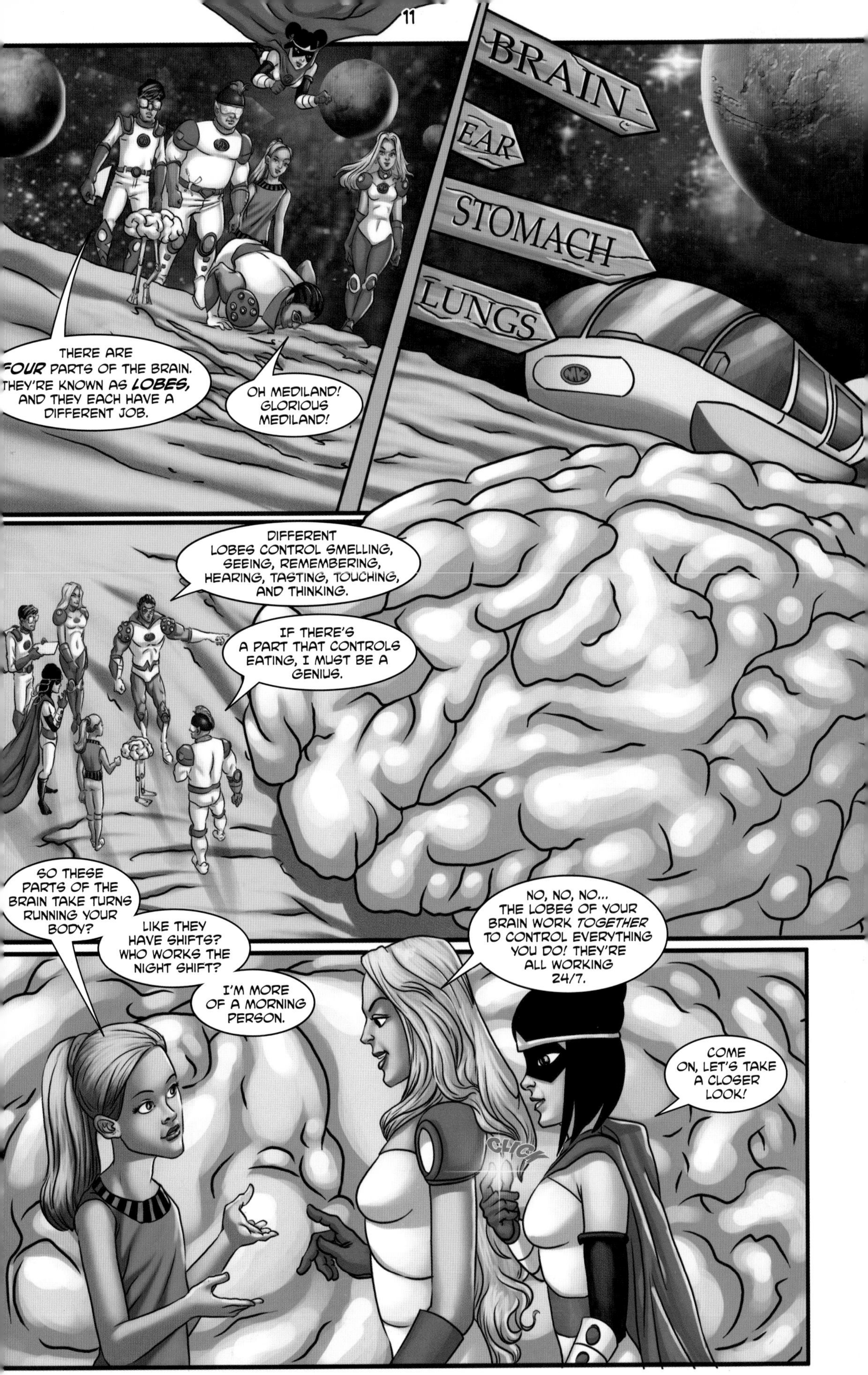
BRAIN
EAR
STOMACH
LUNGS
THERE ARE *FOUR* PARTS OF THE BRAIN. THEY'RE KNOWN AS *LOBES*, AND THEY EACH HAVE A DIFFERENT JOB.
OH MEDILAND! GLORIOUS MEDILAND!
DIFFERENT LOBES CONTROL SMELLING, SEEING, REMEMBERING, HEARING, TASTING, TOUCHING, AND THINKING.
IF THERE'S A PART THAT CONTROLS EATING, I MUST BE A GENIUS.
SO THESE PARTS OF THE BRAIN TAKE TURNS RUNNING YOUR BODY?
LIKE THEY HAVE SHIFTS? WHO WORKS THE NIGHT SHIFT?
I'M MORE OF A MORNING PERSON.
NO, NO, NO... THE LOBES OF YOUR BRAIN WORK *TOGETHER* TO CONTROL EVERYTHING YOU DO! THEY'RE ALL WORKING 24/7.
COME ON, LET'S TAKE A CLOSER LOOK!
CLICK

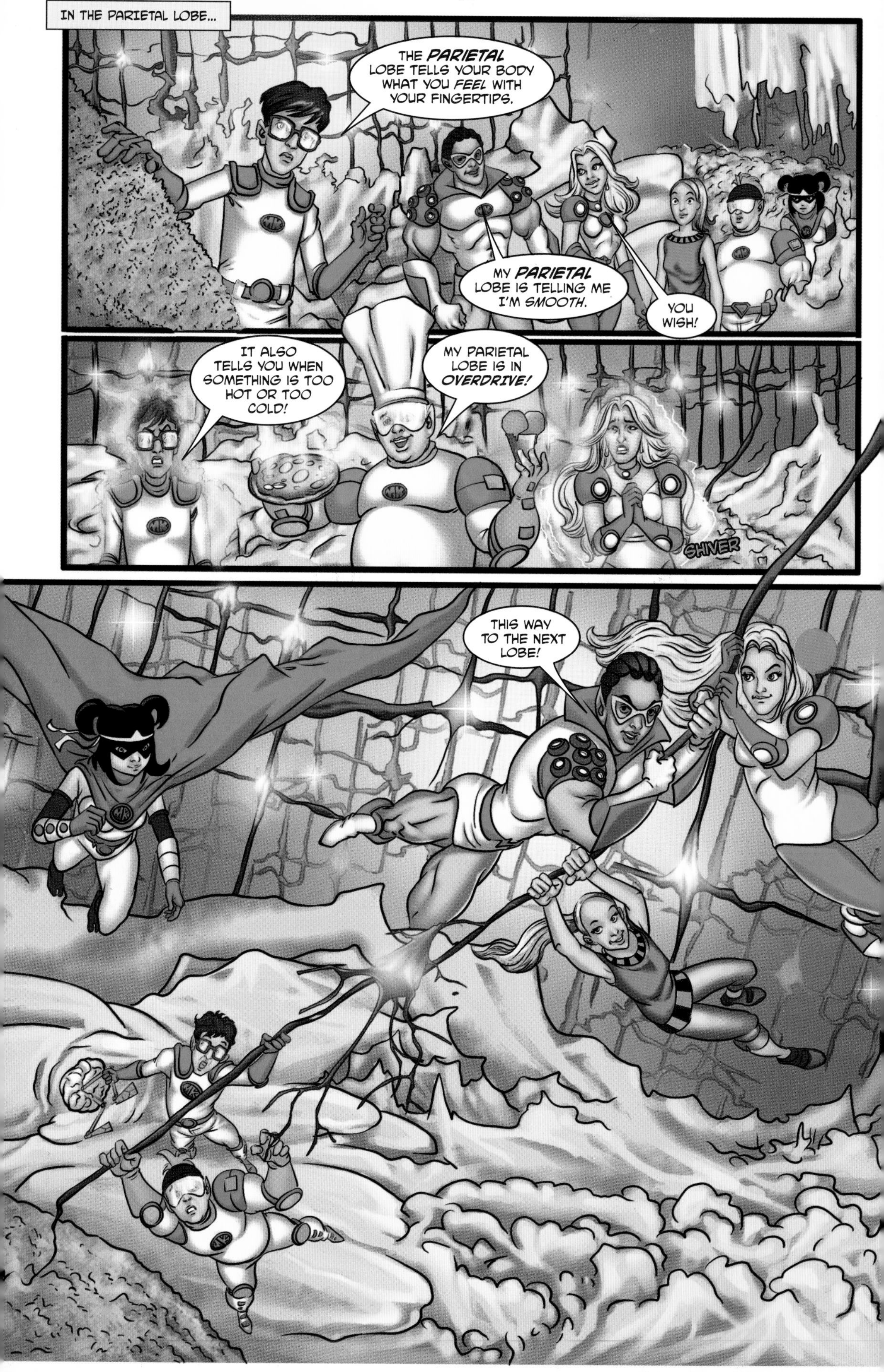
IN THE PARIETAL LOBE...
THE *PARIETAL* LOBE TELLS YOUR BODY WHAT YOU *FEEL* WITH YOUR FINGERTIPS.
MY *PARIETAL* LOBE IS TELLING ME I'M *SMOOTH*.
YOU WISH!
IT ALSO TELLS YOU WHEN SOMETHING IS TOO HOT OR TOO COLD!
MY PARIETAL LOBE IS IN *OVERDRIVE!*
SHIVER
THIS WAY TO THE NEXT LOBE!

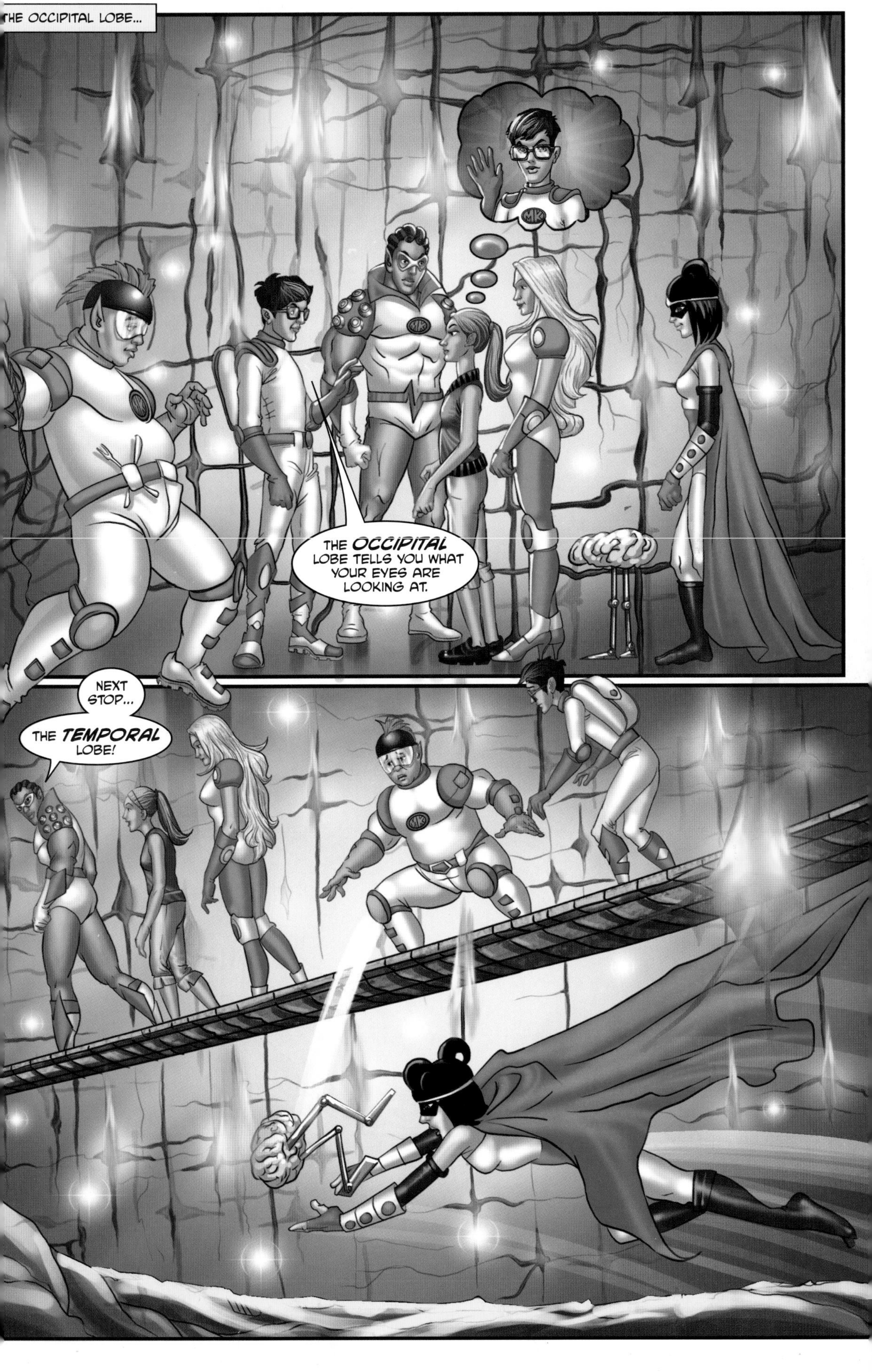
THE OCCIPITAL LOBE...
THE OCCIPITAL LOBE TELLS YOU WHAT YOUR EYES ARE LOOKING AT.
NEXT STOP...
THE TEMPORAL LOBE!

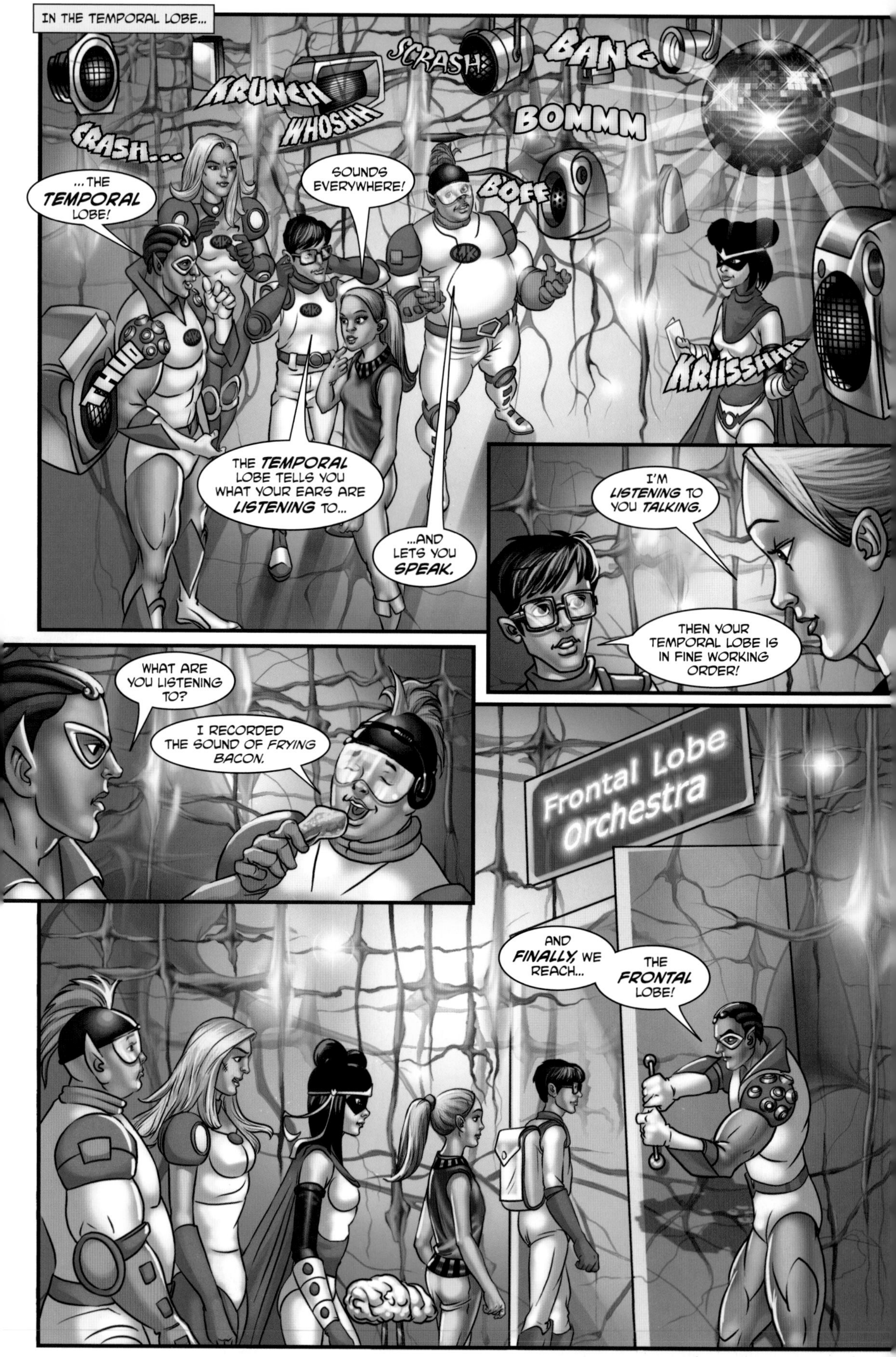
IN THE TEMPORAL LOBE...
KRUNCH
WHOSHH
SCRASH
BANG
BOMMM
CRASH...
...THE TEMPORAL LOBE!
SOUNDS EVERYWHERE!
BOFF
THUD
KRIISSHHH
THE TEMPORAL LOBE TELLS YOU WHAT YOUR EARS ARE LISTENING TO...
...AND LETS YOU SPEAK.
I'M LISTENING TO YOU TALKING.
THEN YOUR TEMPORAL LOBE IS IN FINE WORKING ORDER!
WHAT ARE YOU LISTENING TO?
I RECORDED THE SOUND OF FRYING BACON.
Frontal Lobe Orchestra
AND FINALLY, WE REACH...
THE FRONTAL LOBE!

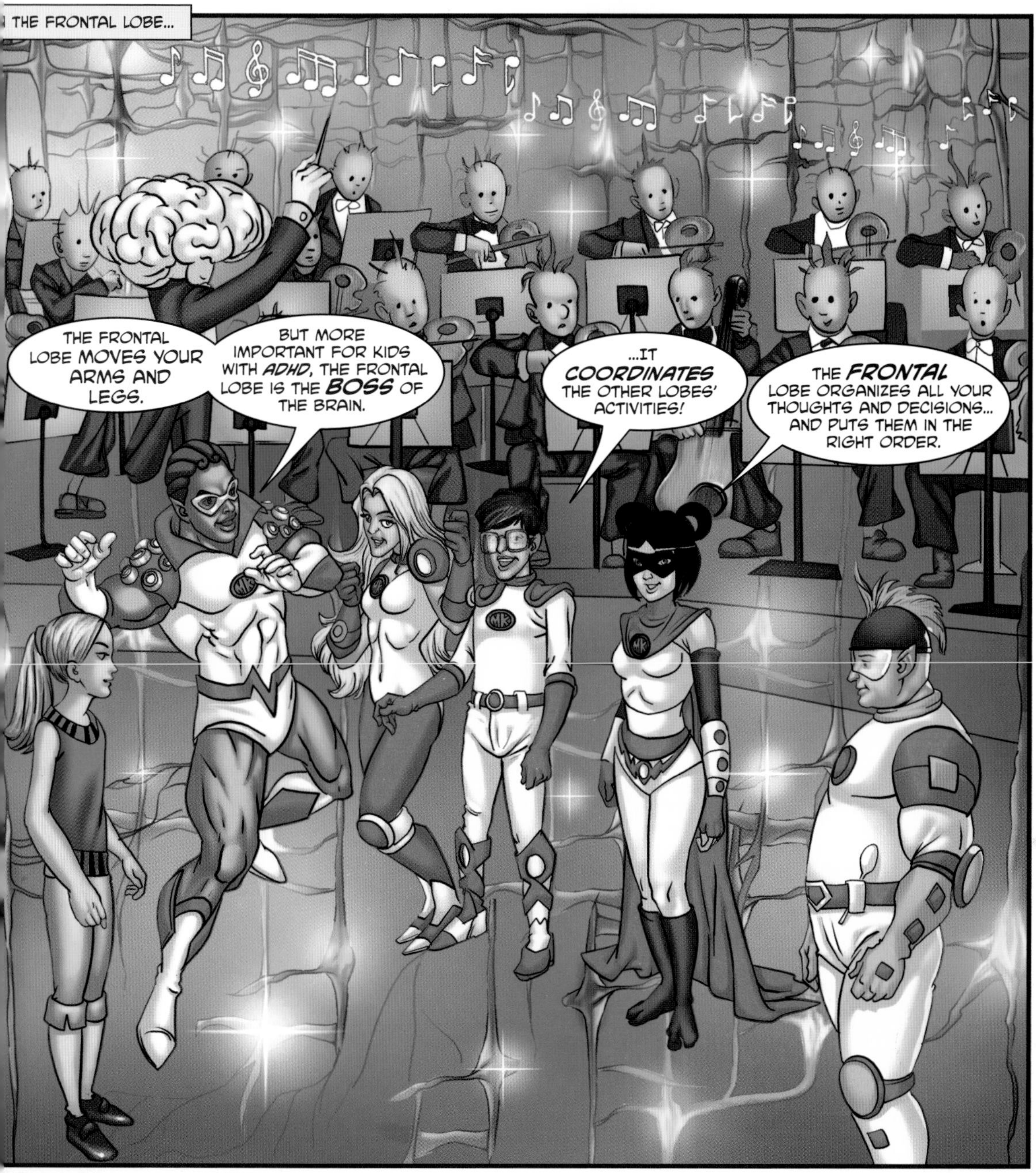
THE FRONTAL LOBE...
THE FRONTAL LOBE MOVES YOUR ARMS AND LEGS.
BUT MORE IMPORTANT FOR KIDS WITH ADHD, THE FRONTAL LOBE IS THE BOSS OF THE BRAIN.
...IT COORDINATES THE OTHER LOBES' ACTIVITIES!
THE FRONTAL LOBE ORGANIZES ALL YOUR THOUGHTS AND DECISIONS... AND PUTS THEM IN THE RIGHT ORDER.

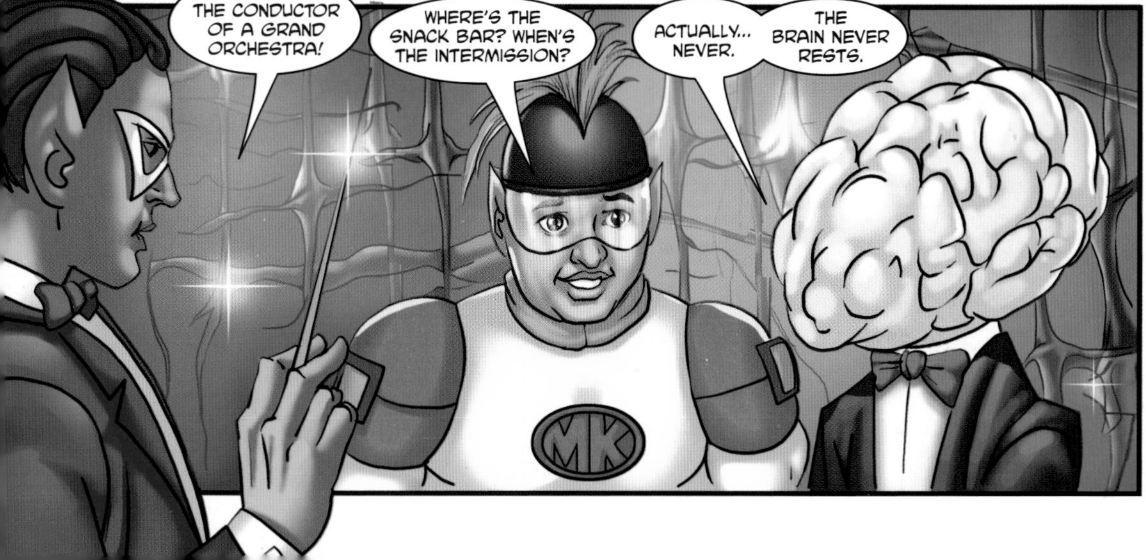
LIKE THE CONDUCTOR OF A GRAND ORCHESTRA!
WHERE'S THE SNACK BAR? WHEN'S THE INTERMISSION?
ACTUALLY... NEVER.
THE BRAIN NEVER RESTS.

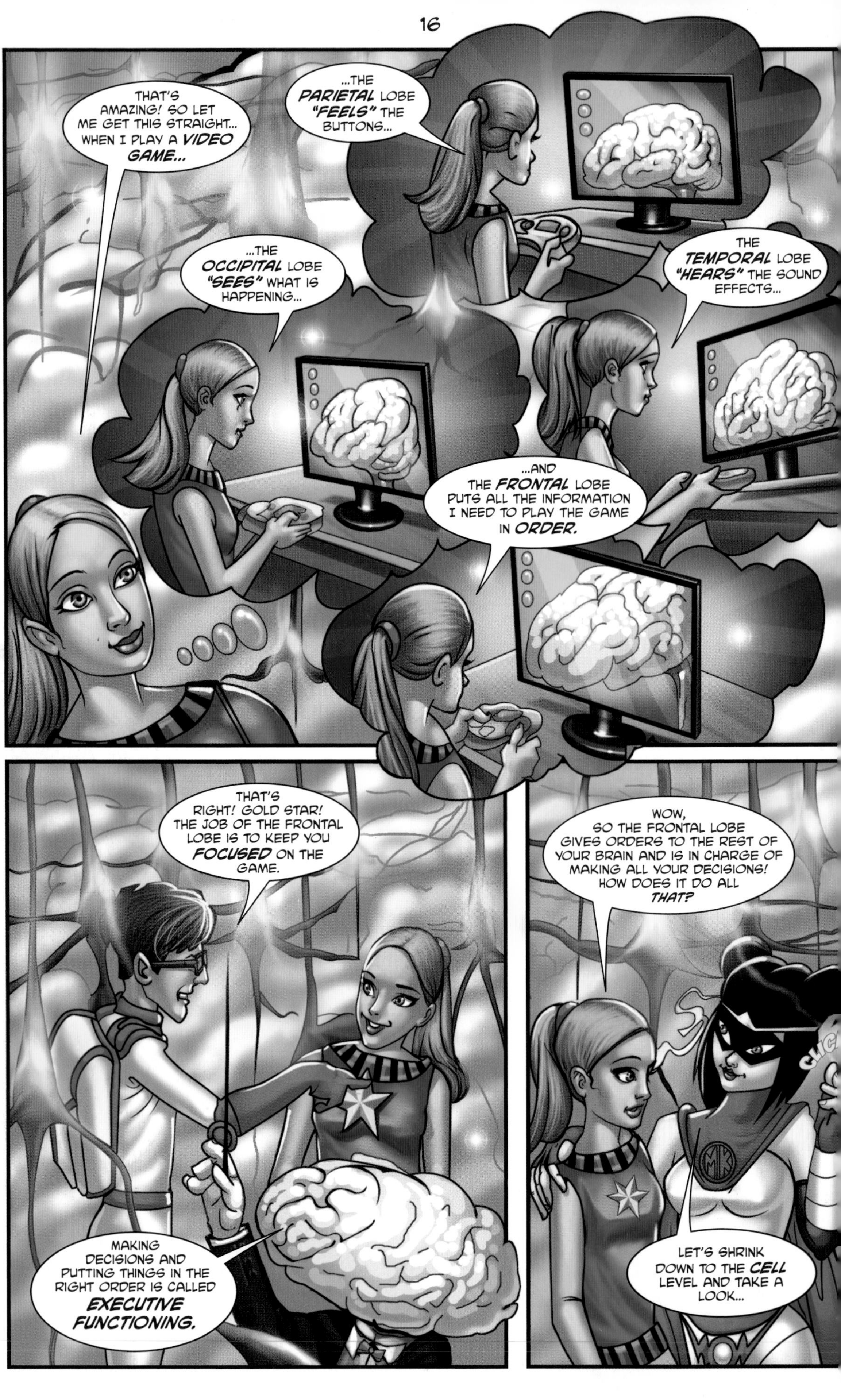
THAT'S AMAZING! SO LET ME GET THIS STRAIGHT... WHEN I PLAY A *VIDEO GAME...*
...THE *PARIETAL* LOBE *"FEELS"* THE BUTTONS...
...THE *OCCIPITAL* LOBE *"SEES"* WHAT IS HAPPENING...
THE *TEMPORAL* LOBE *"HEARS"* THE SOUND EFFECTS...
...AND THE *FRONTAL* LOBE PUTS ALL THE INFORMATION I NEED TO PLAY THE GAME IN *ORDER.*
THAT'S RIGHT! GOLD STAR! THE JOB OF THE FRONTAL LOBE IS TO KEEP YOU *FOCUSED* ON THE GAME.
MAKING DECISIONS AND PUTTING THINGS IN THE RIGHT ORDER IS CALLED *EXECUTIVE FUNCTIONING.*
WOW, SO THE FRONTAL LOBE GIVES ORDERS TO THE REST OF YOUR BRAIN AND IS IN CHARGE OF MAKING ALL YOUR DECISIONS! HOW DOES IT DO ALL *THAT?*
LET'S SHRINK DOWN TO THE *CELL* LEVEL AND TAKE A LOOK...

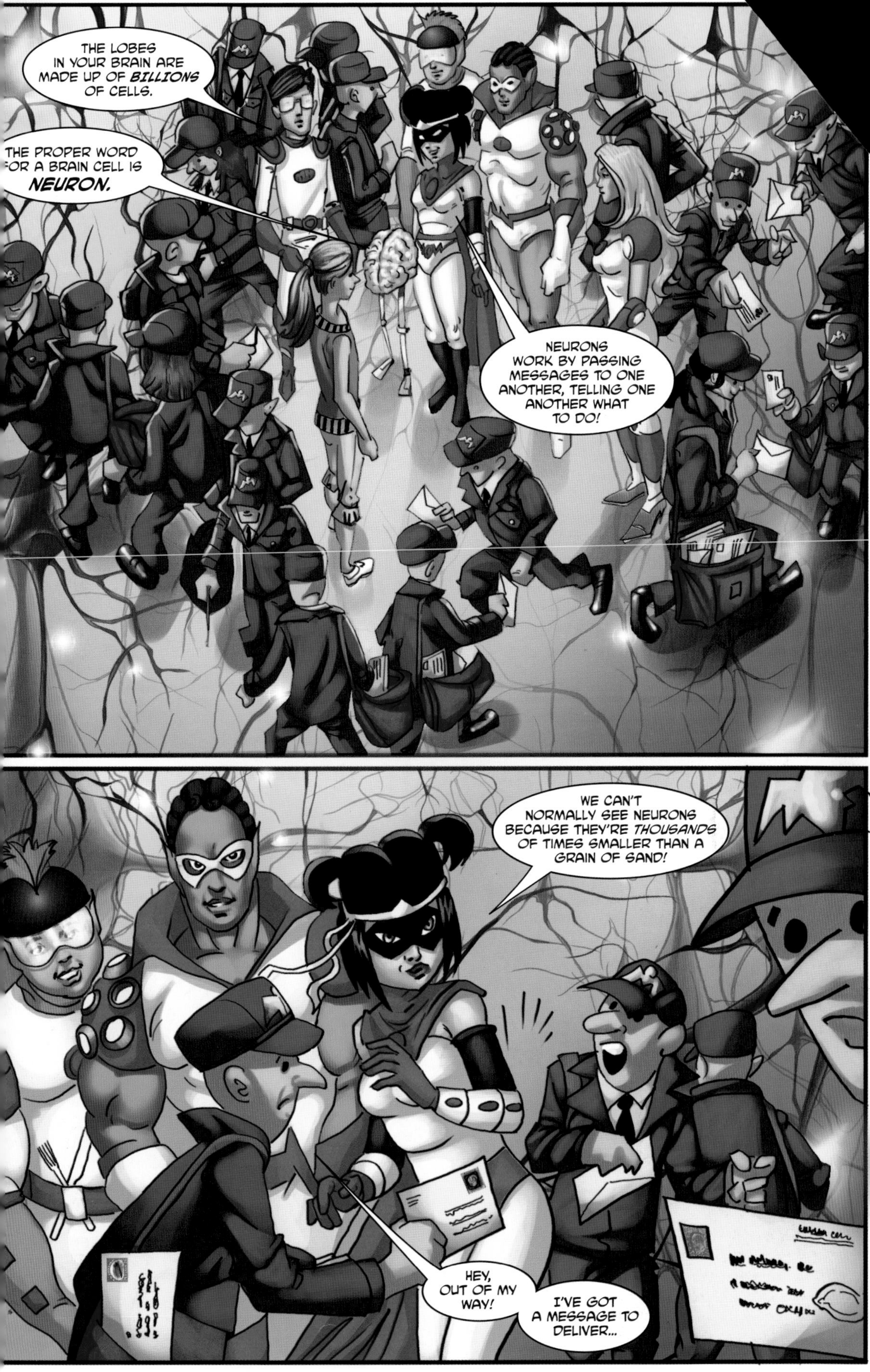
THE LOBES IN YOUR BRAIN ARE MADE UP OF *BILLIONS* OF CELLS.
THE PROPER WORD FOR A BRAIN CELL IS **NEURON.**
NEURONS WORK BY PASSING MESSAGES TO ONE ANOTHER, TELLING ONE ANOTHER WHAT TO DO!
WE CAN'T NORMALLY SEE NEURONS BECAUSE THEY'RE *THOUSANDS* OF TIMES SMALLER THAN A GRAIN OF SAND!
HEY, OUT OF MY WAY!
I'VE GOT A MESSAGE TO DELIVER...

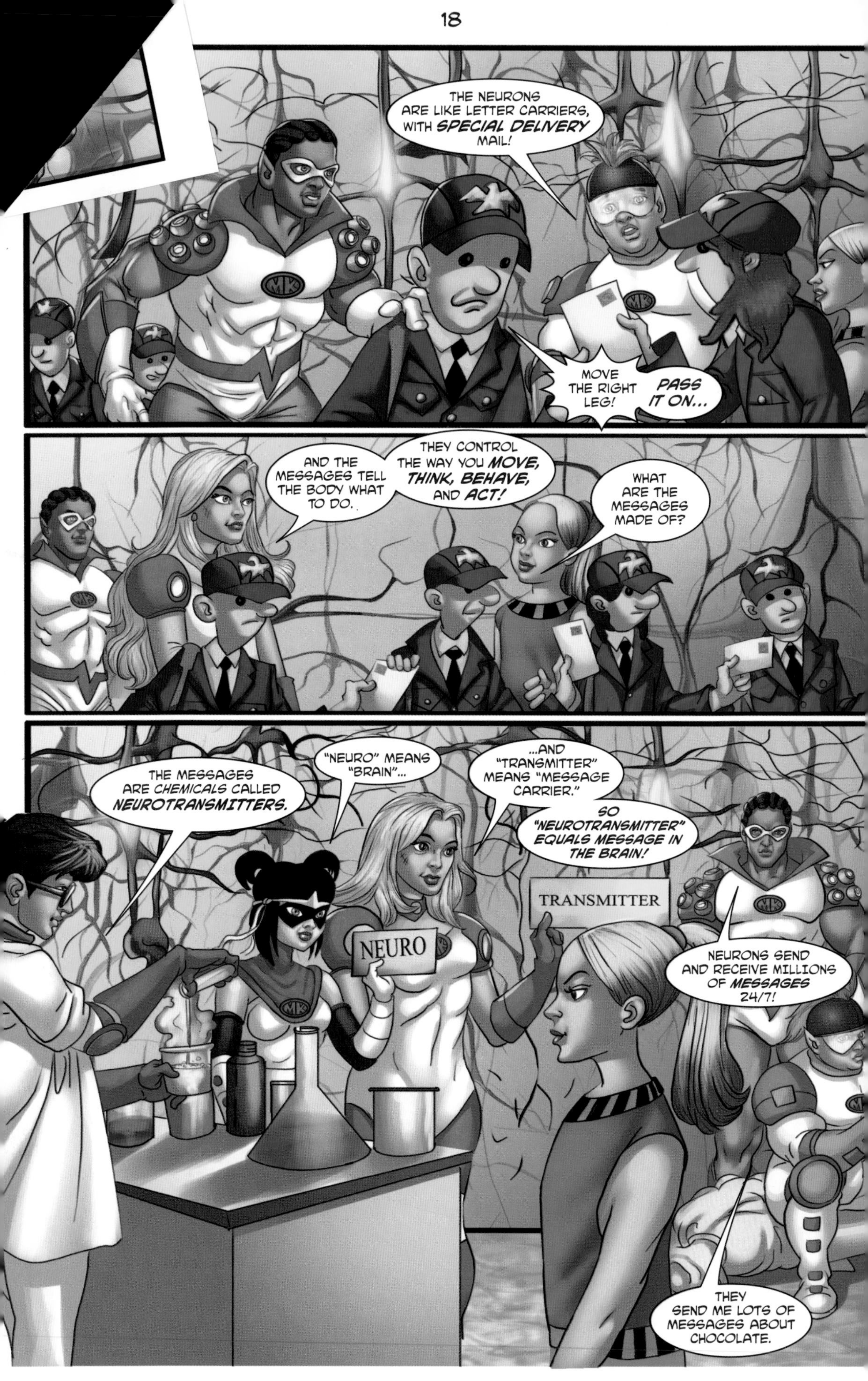
THE NEURONS ARE LIKE LETTER CARRIERS, WITH ***SPECIAL DELIVERY*** MAIL!
MOVE THE RIGHT LEG!
PASS IT ON...
AND THE MESSAGES TELL THE BODY WHAT TO DO.
THEY CONTROL THE WAY YOU ***MOVE, THINK, BEHAVE,*** AND ***ACT!***
WHAT ARE THE MESSAGES MADE OF?
THE MESSAGES ARE *CHEMICALS* CALLED ***NEUROTRANSMITTERS.***
"NEURO" MEANS "BRAIN"...
...AND "TRANSMITTER" MEANS "MESSAGE CARRIER."
SO "NEUROTRANSMITTER" EQUALS MESSAGE IN THE BRAIN!
NEURO
TRANSMITTER
NEURONS SEND AND RECEIVE MILLIONS OF ***MESSAGES*** 24/7!
THEY SEND ME LOTS OF MESSAGES ABOUT CHOCOLATE.

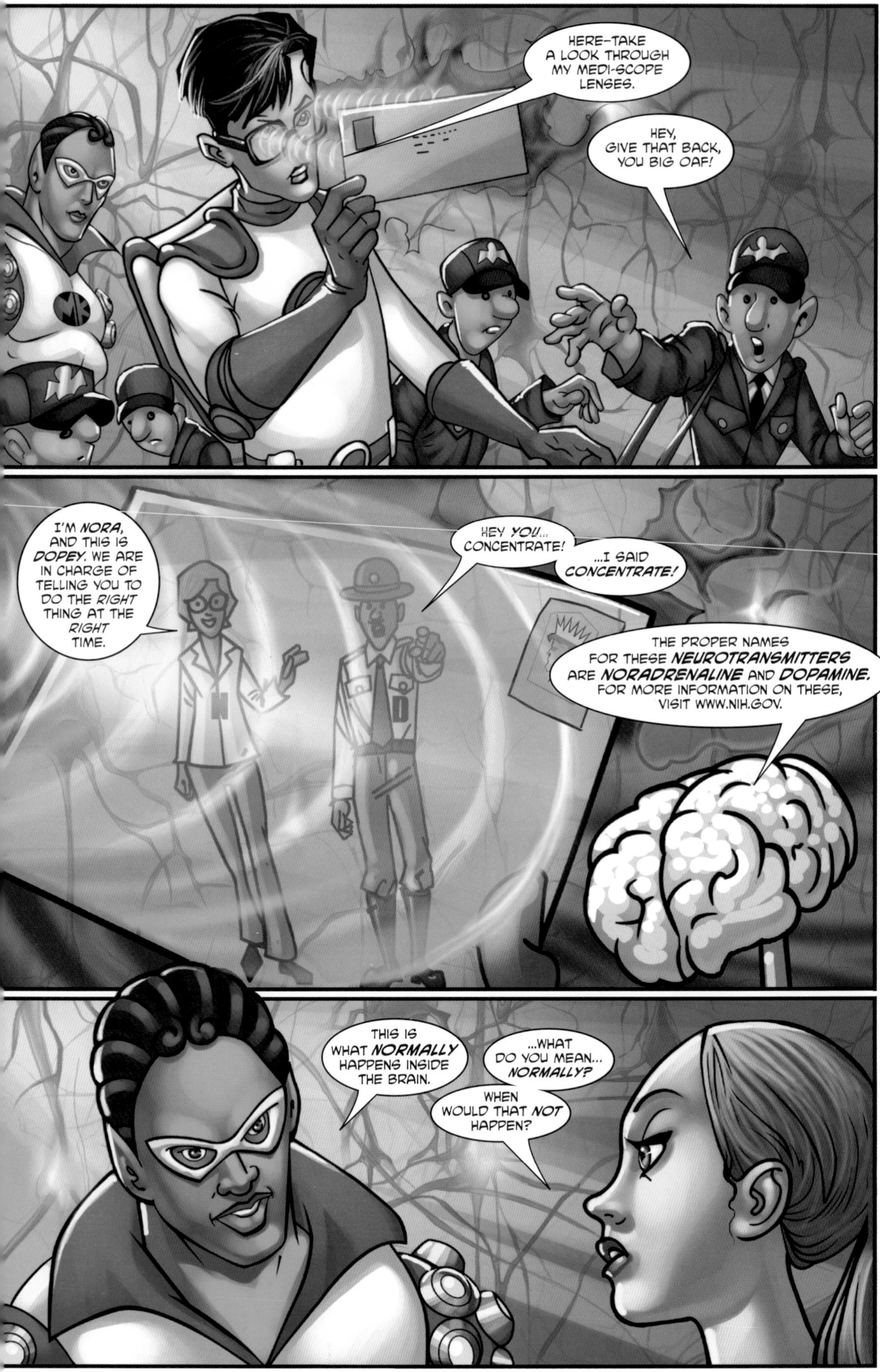
HERE—TAKE A LOOK THROUGH MY MEDI-SCOPE LENSES.
HEY, GIVE THAT BACK, YOU BIG OAF!
I'M NORA, AND THIS IS DOPEY. WE ARE IN CHARGE OF TELLING YOU TO DO THE RIGHT THING AT THE RIGHT TIME.
HEY YOU... CONCENTRATE!
...I SAID CONCENTRATE!
THE PROPER NAMES FOR THESE NEUROTRANSMITTERS ARE NORADRENALINE AND DOPAMINE. FOR MORE INFORMATION ON THESE, VISIT WWW.NIH.GOV.
THIS IS WHAT NORMALLY HAPPENS INSIDE THE BRAIN.
...WHAT DO YOU MEAN... NORMALLY?
WHEN WOULD THAT NOT HAPPEN?

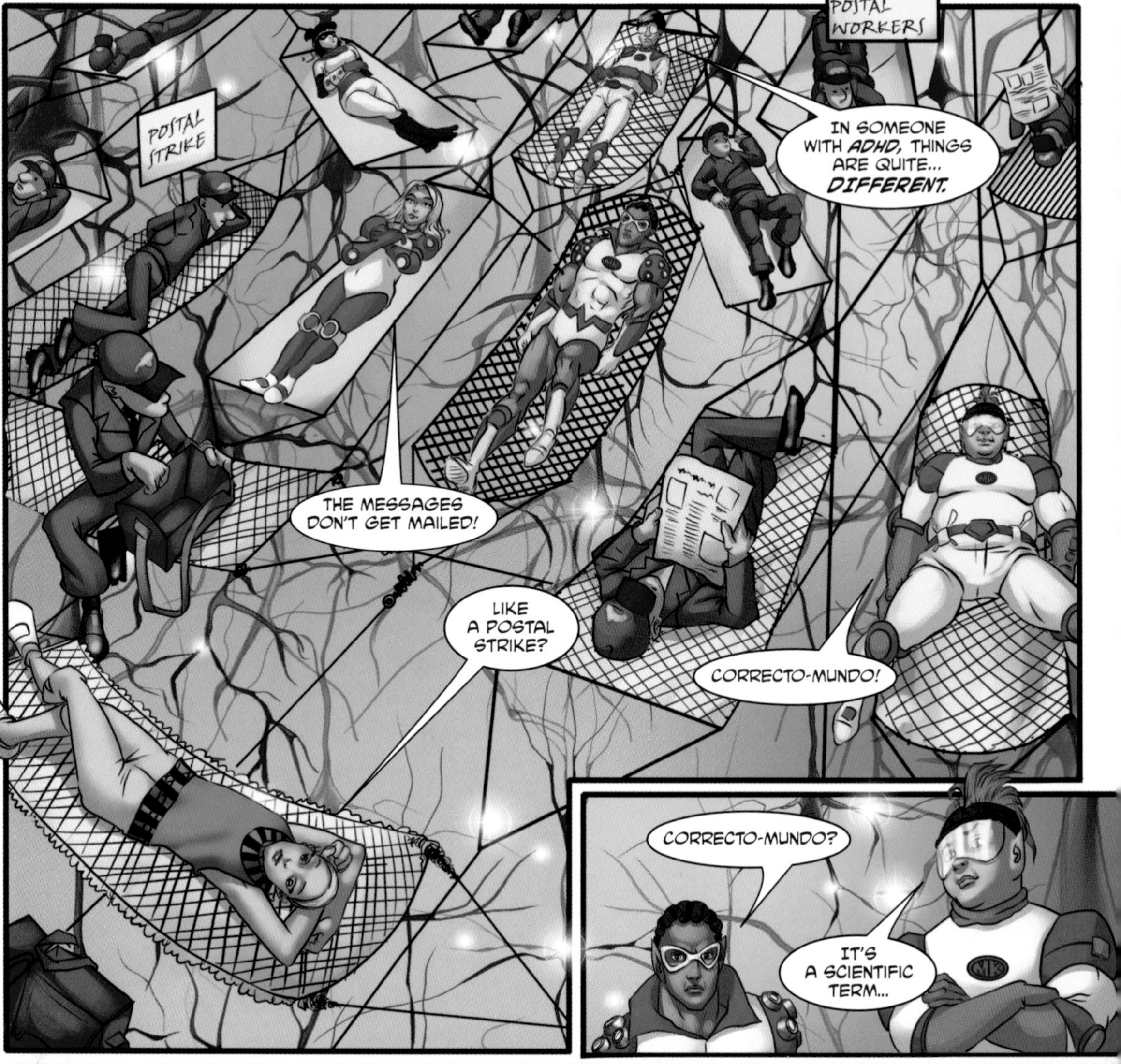
RIGHTS FOR POSTAL WORKERS
POSTAL STRIKE
IN SOMEONE WITH *ADHD,* THINGS ARE QUITE... ***DIFFERENT.***
THE MESSAGES DON'T GET MAILED!
LIKE A POSTAL STRIKE?
CORRECTO-MUNDO!
CORRECTO-MUNDO?
IT'S A SCIENTIFIC TERM...

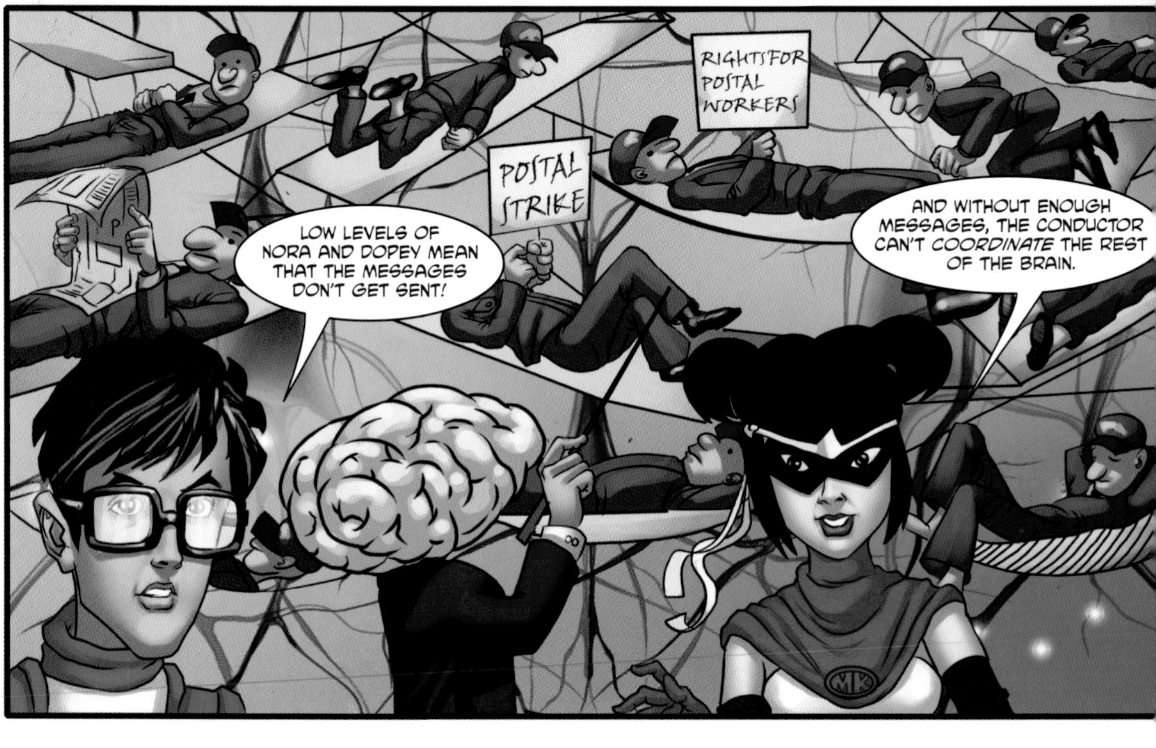
RIGHTS FOR POSTAL WORKERS
POSTAL STRIKE
LOW LEVELS OF NORA AND DOPEY MEAN THAT THE MESSAGES DON'T GET SENT!
AND WITHOUT ENOUGH MESSAGES, THE CONDUCTOR CAN'T *COORDINATE* THE REST OF THE BRAIN.

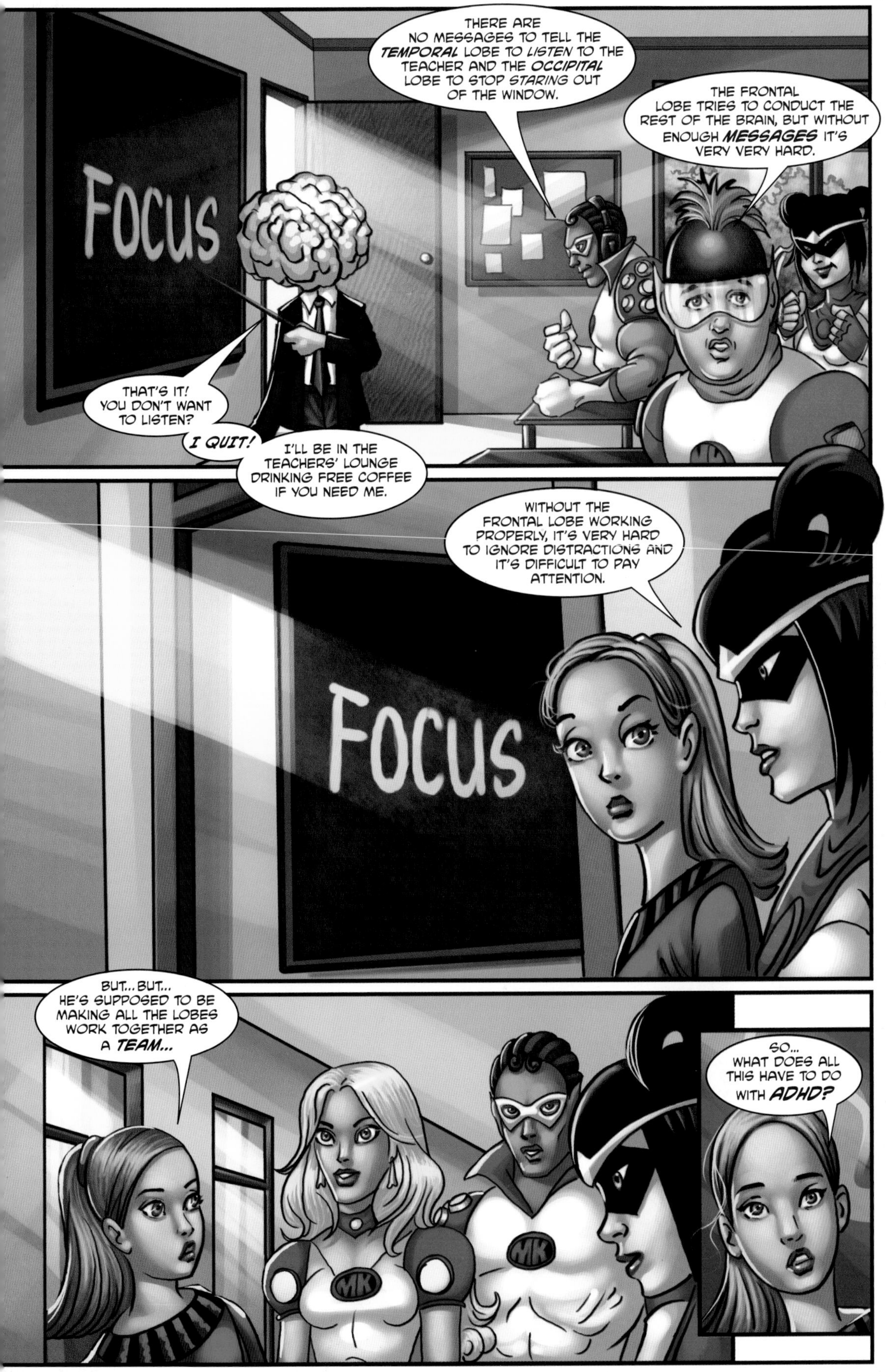
FOCUS
THERE ARE NO MESSAGES TO TELL THE TEMPORAL LOBE TO LISTEN TO THE TEACHER AND THE OCCIPITAL LOBE TO STOP STARING OUT OF THE WINDOW.
THE FRONTAL LOBE TRIES TO CONDUCT THE REST OF THE BRAIN, BUT WITHOUT ENOUGH MESSAGES IT'S VERY VERY HARD.
THAT'S IT! YOU DON'T WANT TO LISTEN?
I QUIT!
I'LL BE IN THE TEACHERS' LOUNGE DRINKING FREE COFFEE IF YOU NEED ME.
WITHOUT THE FRONTAL LOBE WORKING PROPERLY, IT'S VERY HARD TO IGNORE DISTRACTIONS AND IT'S DIFFICULT TO PAY ATTENTION.
FOCUS
BUT...BUT... HE'S SUPPOSED TO BE MAKING ALL THE LOBES WORK TOGETHER AS A TEAM...
SO... WHAT DOES ALL THIS HAVE TO DO WITH ADHD?
MK
MK

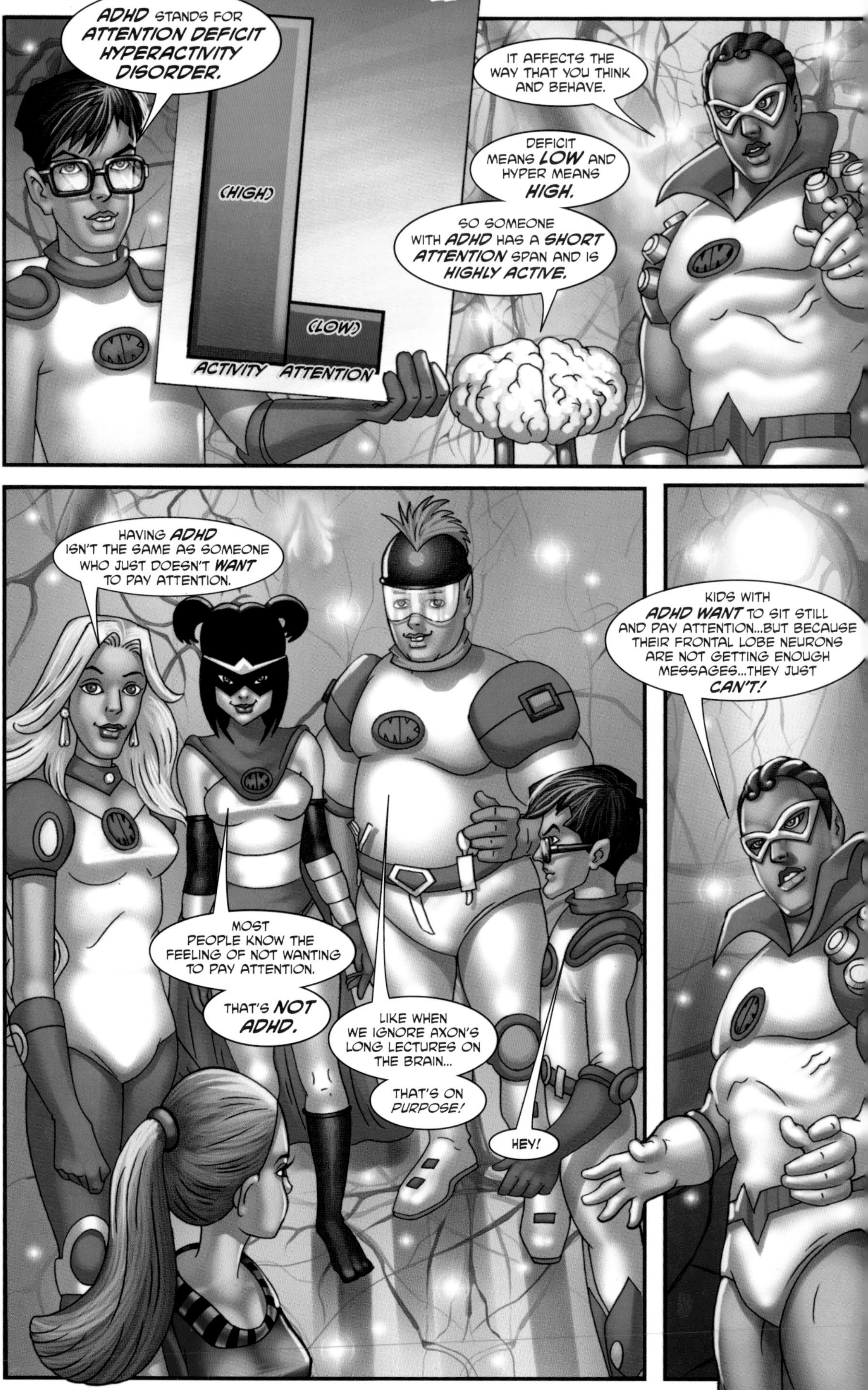
ADHD STANDS FOR ATTENTION DEFICIT HYPERACTIVITY DISORDER.
(HIGH)
(LOW)
ACTIVITY ATTENTION
IT AFFECTS THE WAY THAT YOU THINK AND BEHAVE.
DEFICIT MEANS LOW AND HYPER MEANS HIGH.
SO SOMEONE WITH ADHD HAS A SHORT ATTENTION SPAN AND IS HIGHLY ACTIVE.
HAVING ADHD ISN'T THE SAME AS SOMEONE WHO JUST DOESN'T WANT TO PAY ATTENTION.
MOST PEOPLE KNOW THE FEELING OF NOT WANTING TO PAY ATTENTION.
THAT'S NOT ADHD.
LIKE WHEN WE IGNORE AXON'S LONG LECTURES ON THE BRAIN...
THAT'S ON PURPOSE!
HEY!
KIDS WITH ADHD WANT TO SIT STILL AND PAY ATTENTION...BUT BECAUSE THEIR FRONTAL LOBE NEURONS ARE NOT GETTING ENOUGH MESSAGES...THEY JUST CAN'T!

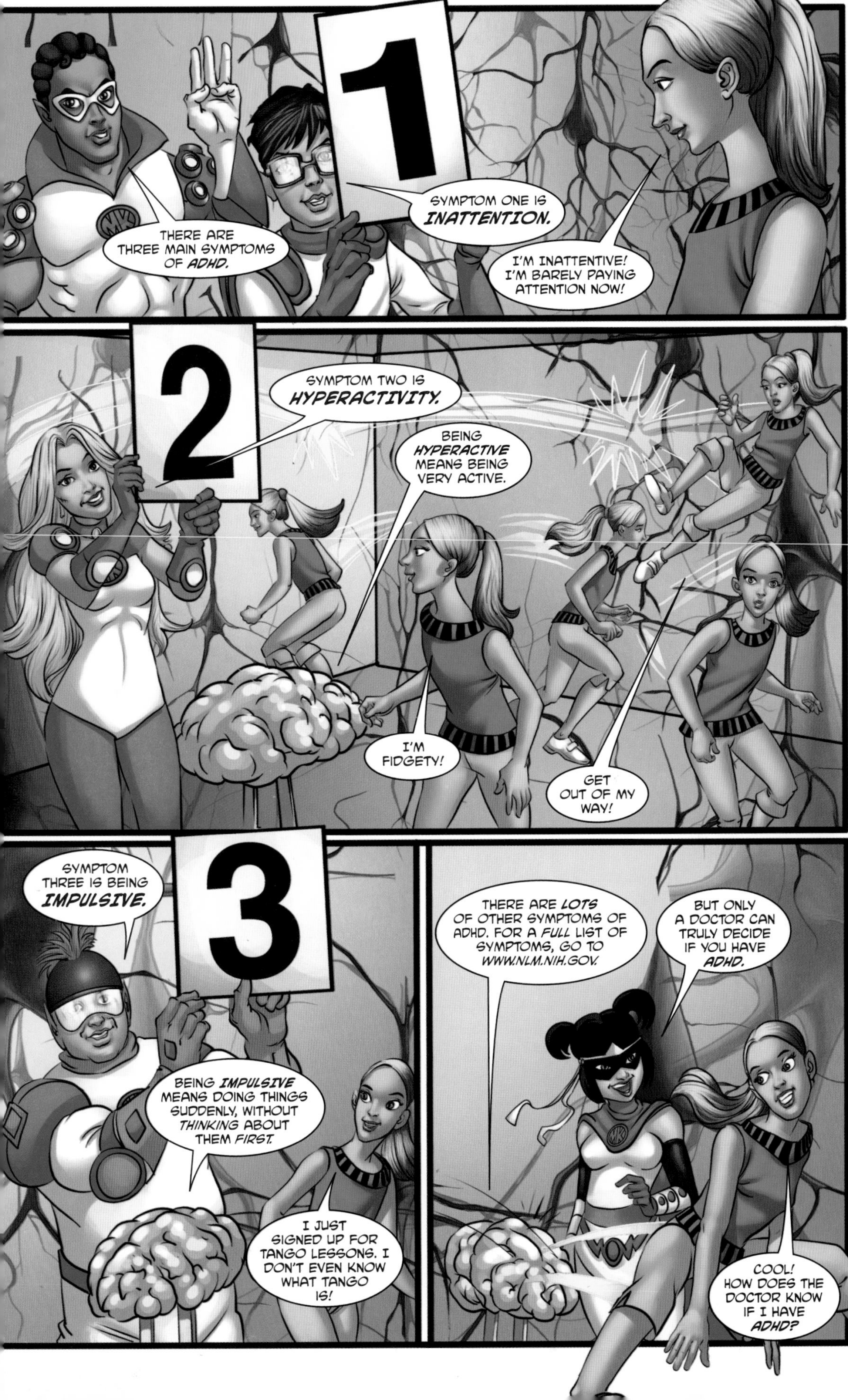
1
THERE ARE THREE MAIN SYMPTOMS OF ADHD.
SYMPTOM ONE IS INATTENTION.
I'M INATTENTIVE! I'M BARELY PAYING ATTENTION NOW!
2
SYMPTOM TWO IS HYPERACTIVITY.
BEING HYPERACTIVE MEANS BEING VERY ACTIVE.
I'M FIDGETY!
GET OUT OF MY WAY!
SYMPTOM THREE IS BEING IMPULSIVE.
3
BEING IMPULSIVE MEANS DOING THINGS SUDDENLY, WITHOUT THINKING ABOUT THEM FIRST.
I JUST SIGNED UP FOR TANGO LESSONS. I DON'T EVEN KNOW WHAT TANGO IS!
THERE ARE LOTS OF OTHER SYMPTOMS OF ADHD. FOR A FULL LIST OF SYMPTOMS, GO TO WWW.NLM.NIH.GOV.
BUT ONLY A DOCTOR CAN TRULY DECIDE IF YOU HAVE ADHD.
COOL! HOW DOES THE DOCTOR KNOW IF I HAVE ADHD?

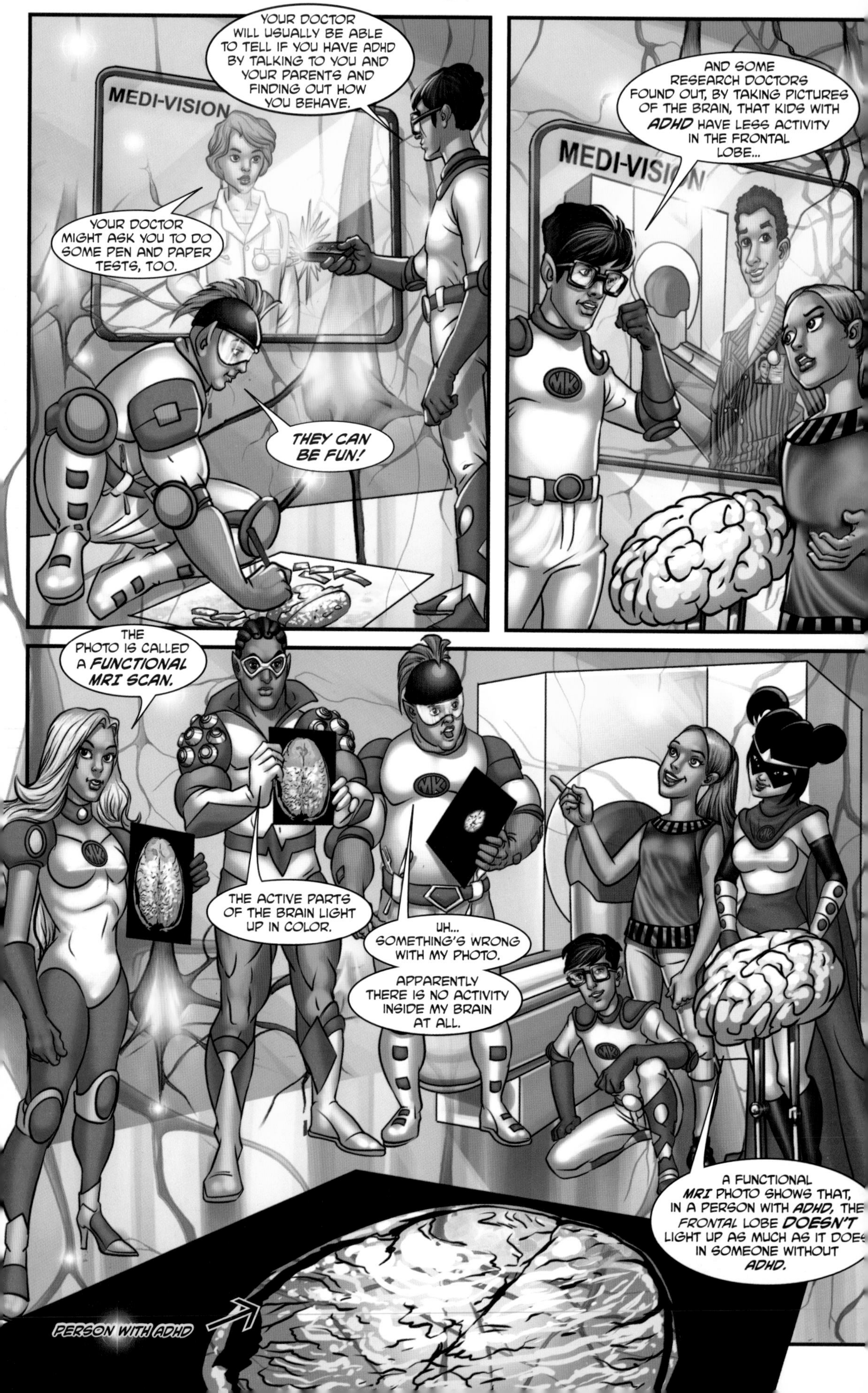

YOUR DOCTOR WILL USUALLY BE ABLE TO TELL IF YOU HAVE ADHD BY TALKING TO YOU AND YOUR PARENTS AND FINDING OUT HOW YOU BEHAVE.
MEDI-VISION
YOUR DOCTOR MIGHT ASK YOU TO DO SOME PEN AND PAPER TESTS, TOO.
THEY CAN BE FUN!
AND SOME RESEARCH DOCTORS FOUND OUT, BY TAKING PICTURES OF THE BRAIN, THAT KIDS WITH ADHD HAVE LESS ACTIVITY IN THE FRONTAL LOBE...
MEDI-VISION
THE PHOTO IS CALLED A FUNCTIONAL MRI SCAN.
THE ACTIVE PARTS OF THE BRAIN LIGHT UP IN COLOR.
UH... SOMETHING'S WRONG WITH MY PHOTO.
APPARENTLY THERE IS NO ACTIVITY INSIDE MY BRAIN AT ALL.
A FUNCTIONAL MRI PHOTO SHOWS THAT, IN A PERSON WITH ADHD, THE FRONTAL LOBE DOESN'T LIGHT UP AS MUCH AS IT DOES IN SOMEONE WITHOUT ADHD.
PERSON WITH ADHD

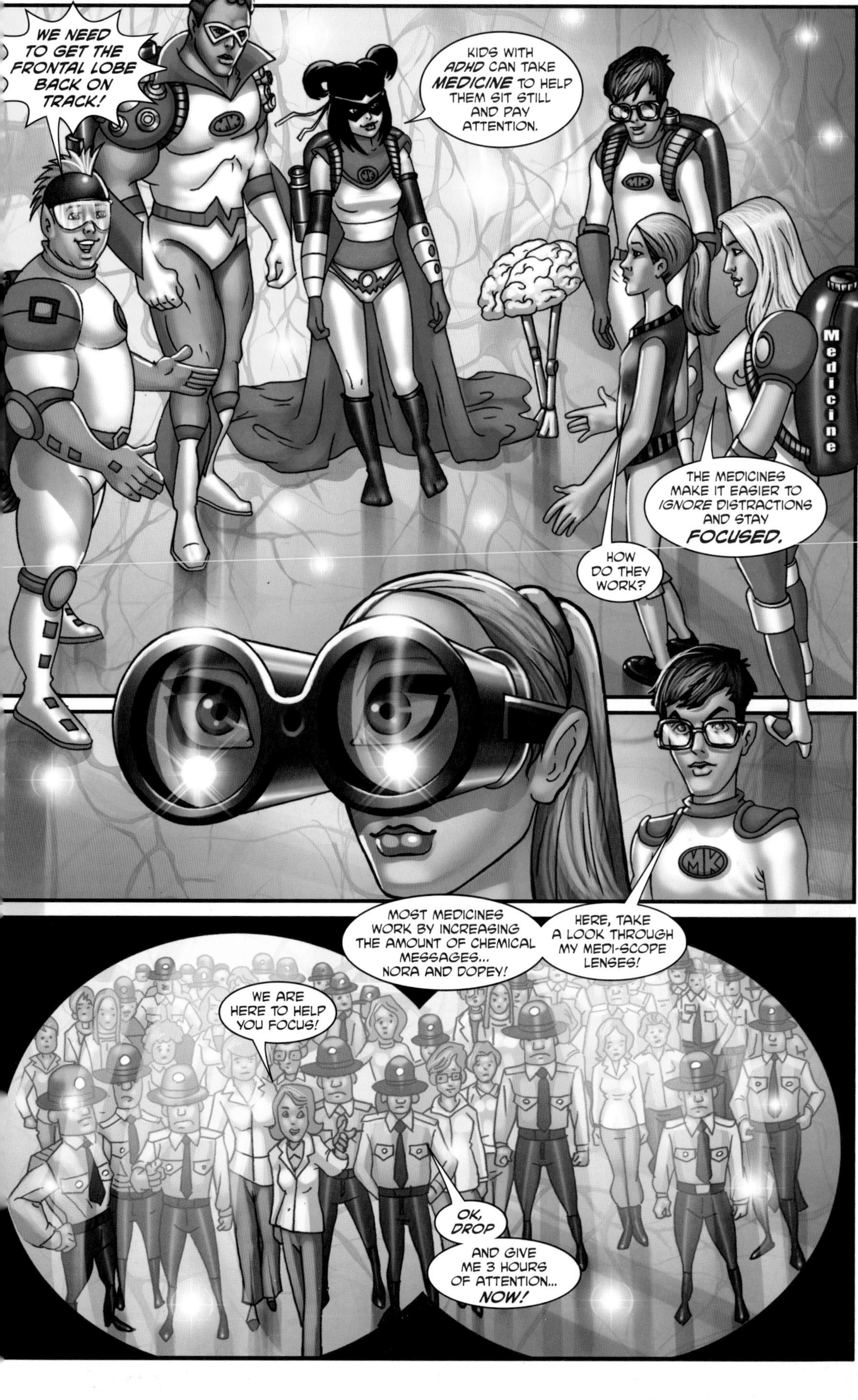
WE NEED TO GET THE FRONTAL LOBE BACK ON TRACK!
KIDS WITH *ADHD* CAN TAKE **MEDICINE** TO HELP THEM SIT STILL AND PAY ATTENTION.
Medicine
THE MEDICINES MAKE IT EASIER TO *IGNORE* DISTRACTIONS AND STAY **FOCUSED.**
HOW DO THEY WORK?
HERE, TAKE A LOOK THROUGH MY MEDI-SCOPE LENSES!
MOST MEDICINES WORK BY INCREASING THE AMOUNT OF CHEMICAL MESSAGES... NORA AND DOPEY!
WE ARE HERE TO HELP YOU FOCUS!
OK, DROP
AND GIVE ME 3 HOURS OF ATTENTION... **NOW!**

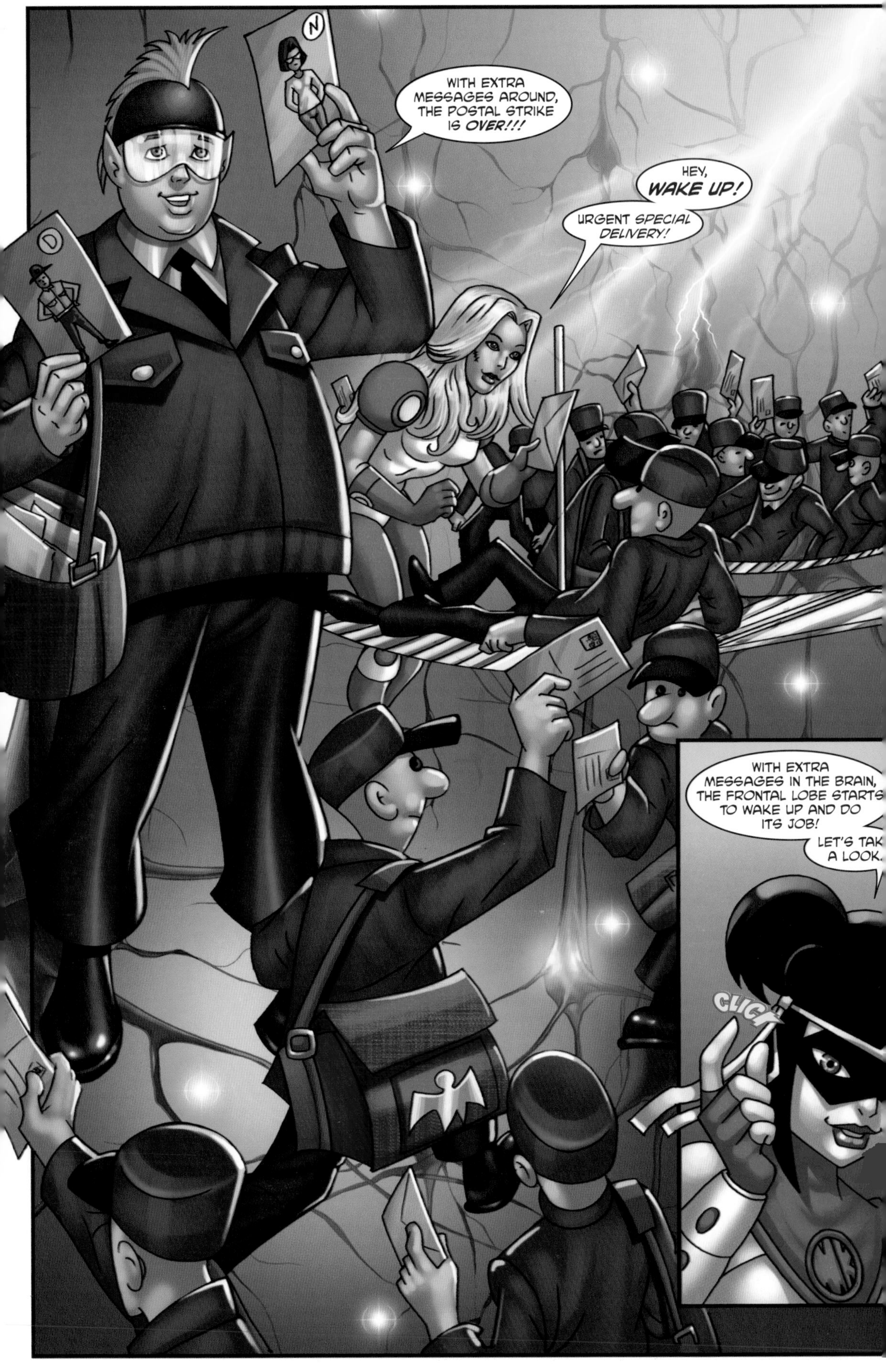
WITH EXTRA MESSAGES AROUND, THE POSTAL STRIKE IS *OVER!!!*
HEY, **WAKE UP!**
URGENT SPECIAL DELIVERY!
WITH EXTRA MESSAGES IN THE BRAIN, THE FRONTAL LOBE STARTS TO WAKE UP AND DO ITS JOB!
LET'S TAK A LOOK.
CLICK

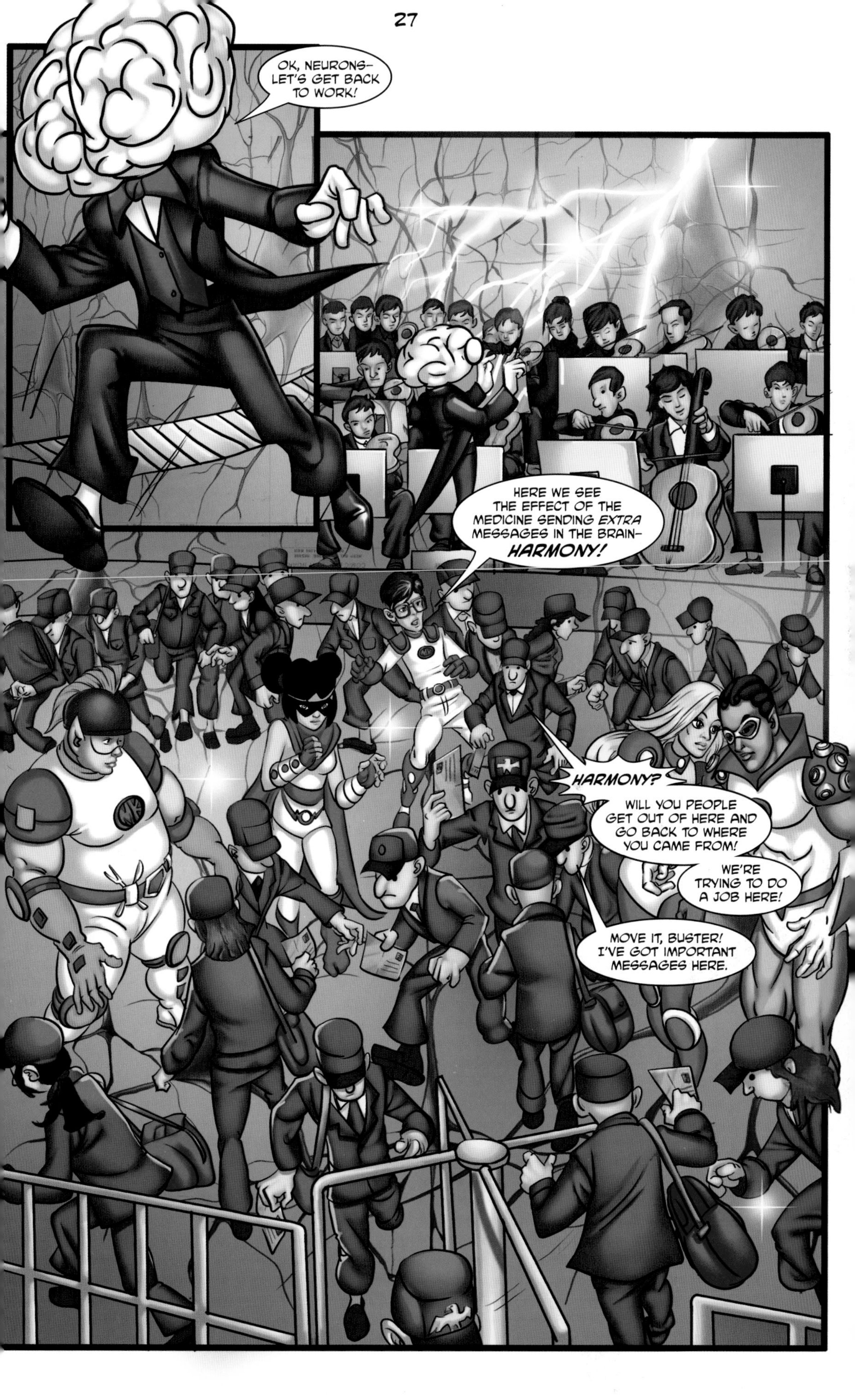
OK, NEURONS- LET'S GET BACK TO WORK!
HERE WE SEE THE EFFECT OF THE MEDICINE SENDING *EXTRA* MESSAGES IN THE BRAIN- **HARMONY!**
HARMONY?
WILL YOU PEOPLE GET OUT OF HERE AND GO BACK TO WHERE YOU CAME FROM!
WE'RE TRYING TO DO A JOB HERE!
MOVE IT, BUSTER! I'VE GOT IMPORTANT MESSAGES HERE.

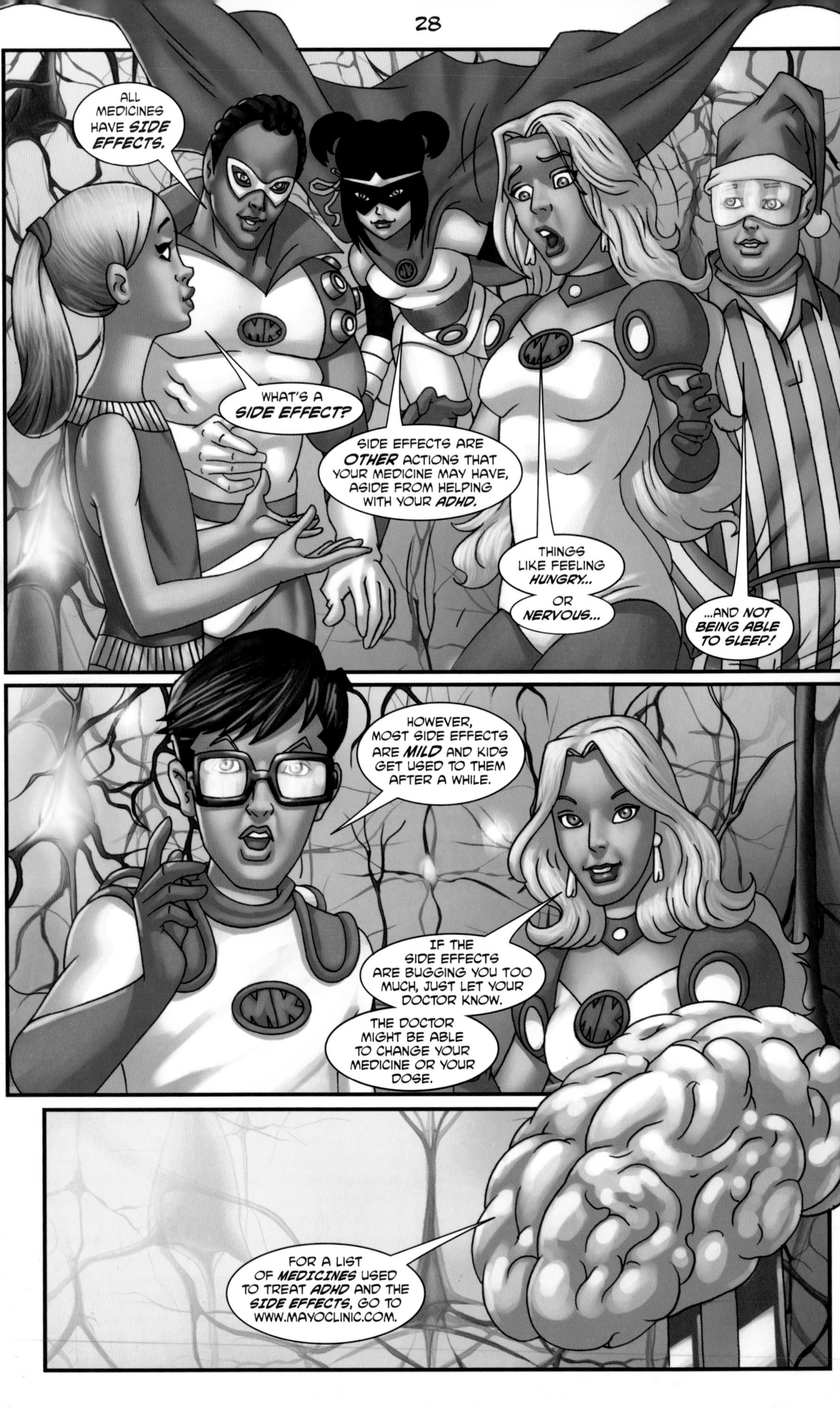
ALL MEDICINES HAVE SIDE EFFECTS.
WHAT'S A SIDE EFFECT?
SIDE EFFECTS ARE OTHER ACTIONS THAT YOUR MEDICINE MAY HAVE, ASIDE FROM HELPING WITH YOUR ADHD.
THINGS LIKE FEELING HUNGRY...
OR NERVOUS...
...AND NOT BEING ABLE TO SLEEP!
HOWEVER, MOST SIDE EFFECTS ARE MILD AND KIDS GET USED TO THEM AFTER A WHILE.
IF THE SIDE EFFECTS ARE BUGGING YOU TOO MUCH, JUST LET YOUR DOCTOR KNOW.
THE DOCTOR MIGHT BE ABLE TO CHANGE YOUR MEDICINE OR YOUR DOSE.
FOR A LIST OF MEDICINES USED TO TREAT ADHD AND THE SIDE EFFECTS, GO TO WWW.MAYOCLINIC.COM.

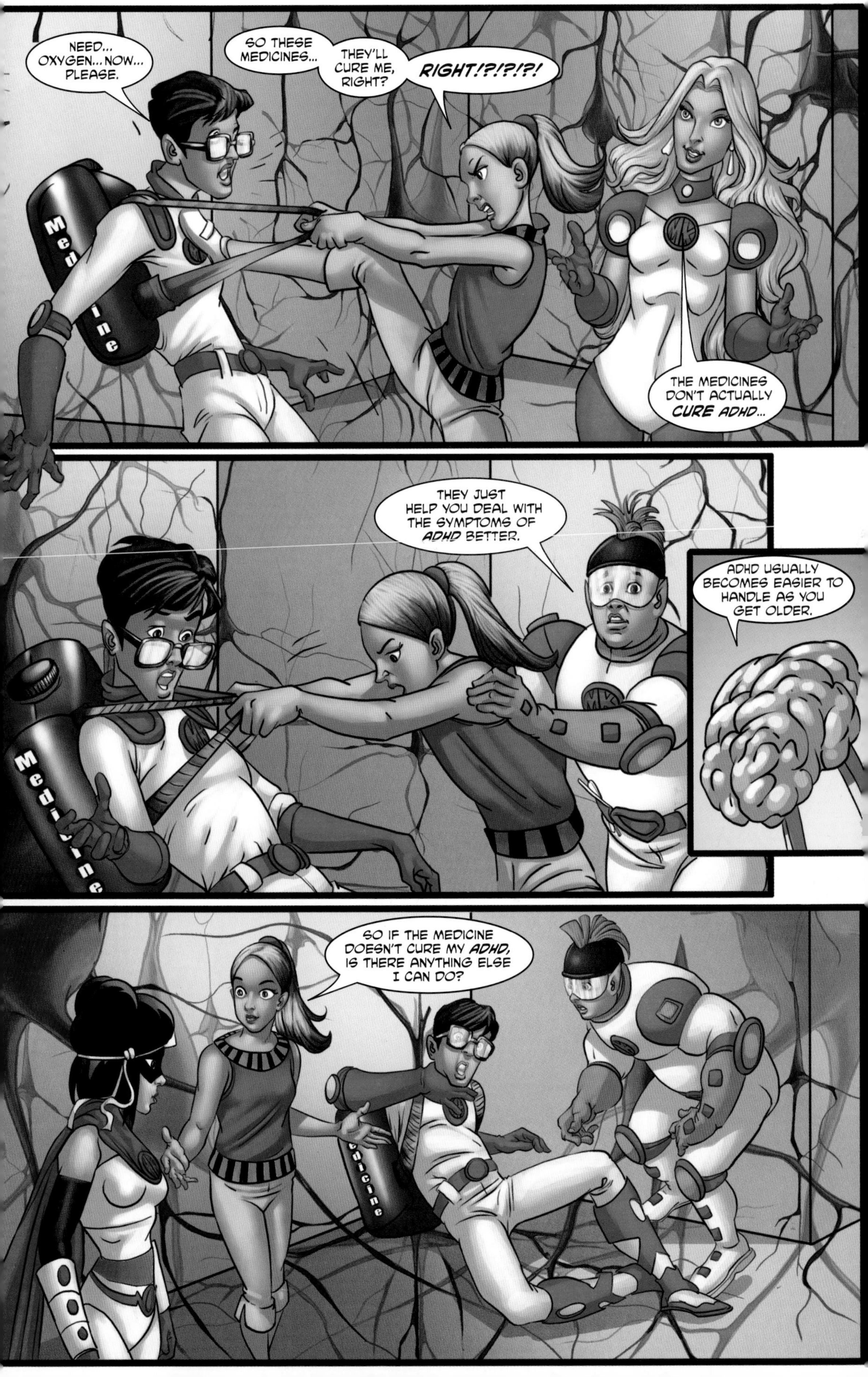
NEED... OXYGEN... NOW... PLEASE.
SO THESE MEDICINES...
THEY'LL CURE ME, RIGHT?
RIGHT!?!?!?!
THE MEDICINES DON'T ACTUALLY CURE ADHD...
THEY JUST HELP YOU DEAL WITH THE SYMPTOMS OF ADHD BETTER.
ADHD USUALLY BECOMES EASIER TO HANDLE AS YOU GET OLDER.
SO IF THE MEDICINE DOESN'T CURE MY ADHD, IS THERE ANYTHING ELSE I CAN DO?

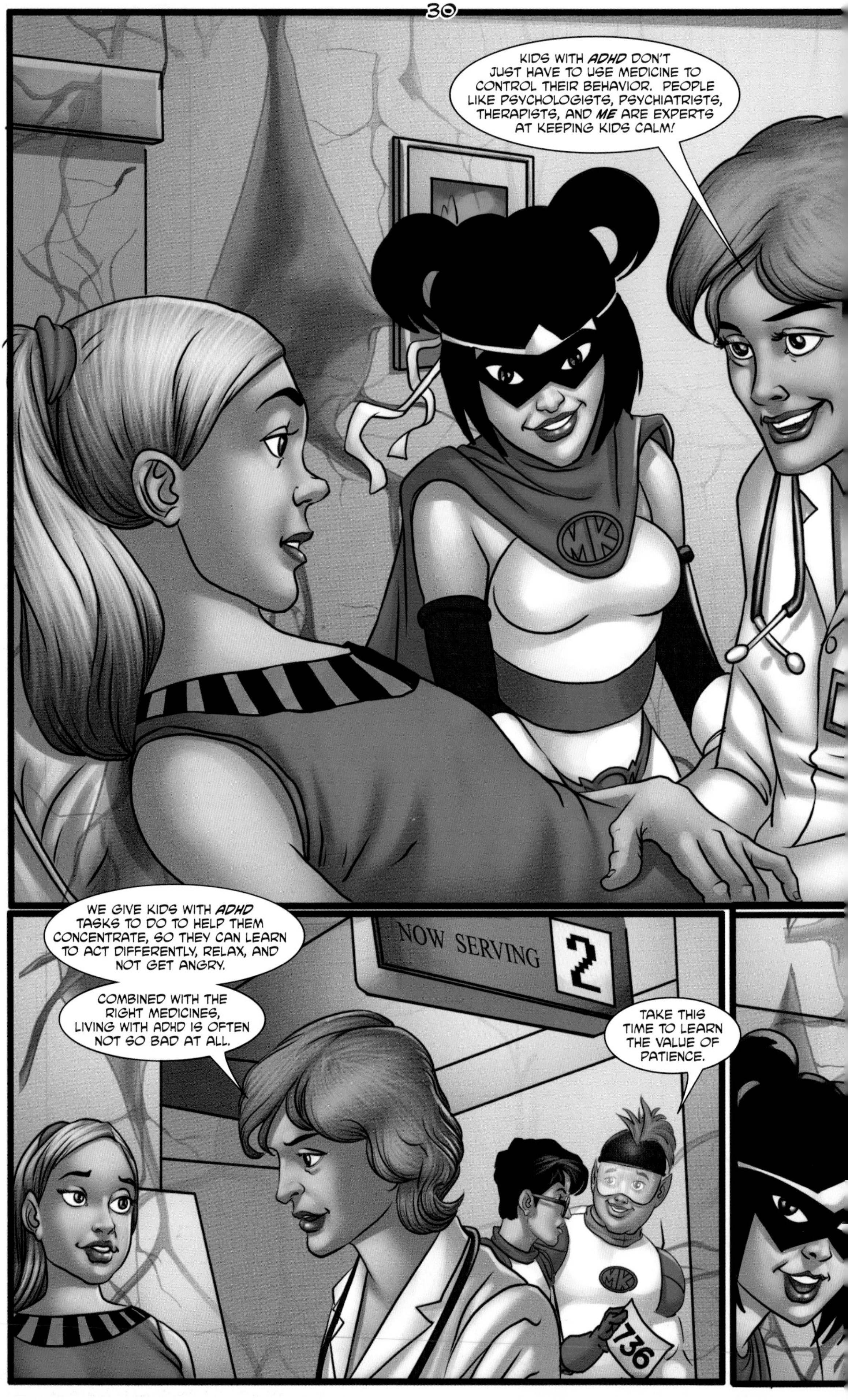
KIDS WITH ADHD DON'T JUST HAVE TO USE MEDICINE TO CONTROL THEIR BEHAVIOR. PEOPLE LIKE PSYCHOLOGISTS, PSYCHIATRISTS, THERAPISTS, AND ME ARE EXPERTS AT KEEPING KIDS CALM!
WE GIVE KIDS WITH ADHD TASKS TO DO TO HELP THEM CONCENTRATE, SO THEY CAN LEARN TO ACT DIFFERENTLY, RELAX, AND NOT GET ANGRY.
COMBINED WITH THE RIGHT MEDICINES, LIVING WITH ADHD IS OFTEN NOT SO BAD AT ALL.
NOW SERVING 2
TAKE THIS TIME TO LEARN THE VALUE OF PATIENCE.
736

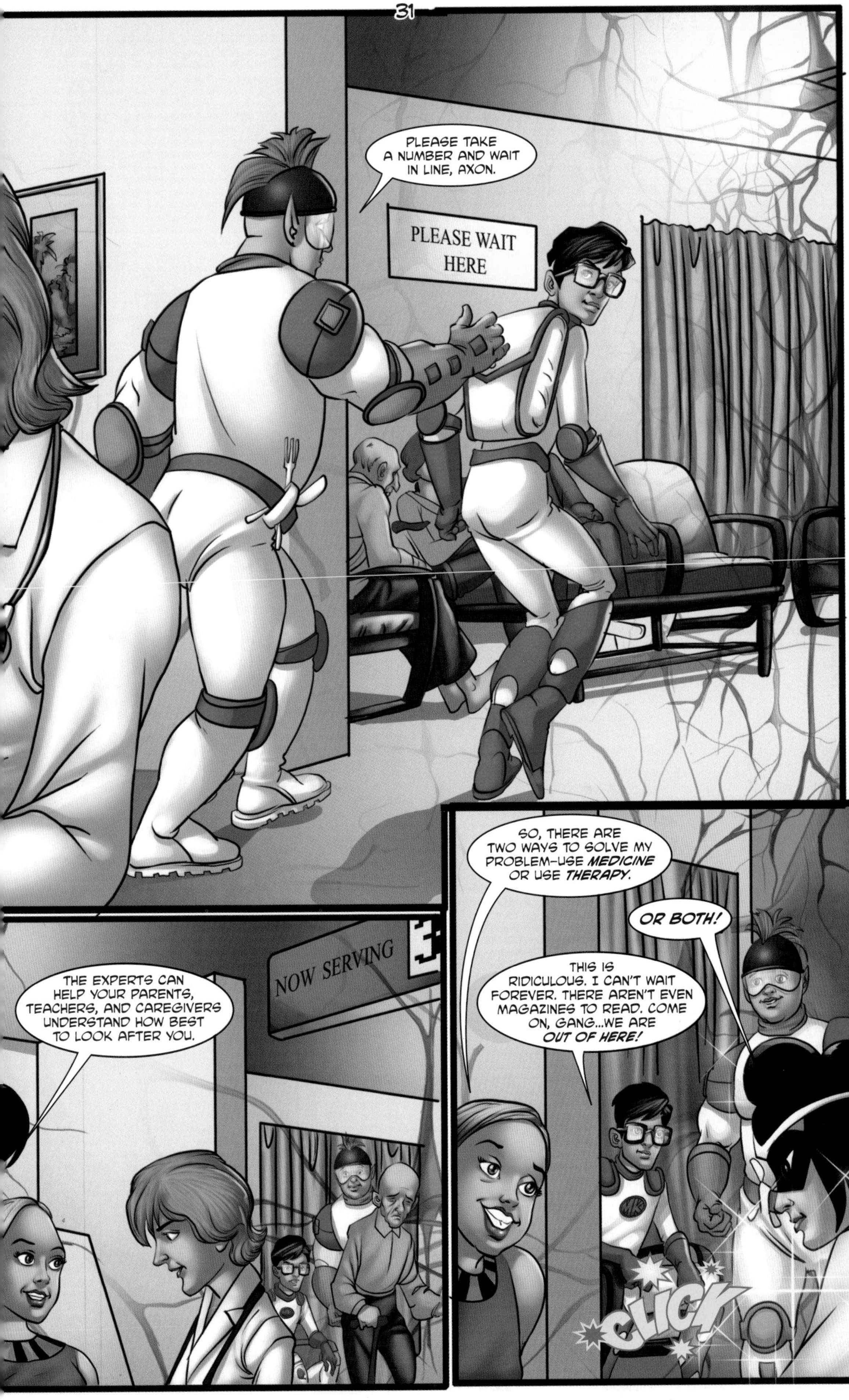
PLEASE TAKE A NUMBER AND WAIT IN LINE, AXON.
PLEASE WAIT HERE
NOW SERVING
THE EXPERTS CAN HELP YOUR PARENTS, TEACHERS, AND CAREGIVERS UNDERSTAND HOW BEST TO LOOK AFTER YOU.
SO, THERE ARE TWO WAYS TO SOLVE MY PROBLEM–USE *MEDICINE* OR USE *THERAPY*.
OR BOTH!
THIS IS RIDICULOUS. I CAN'T WAIT FOREVER. THERE AREN'T EVEN MAGAZINES TO READ. COME ON, GANG...WE ARE *OUT OF HERE!*
CLICK

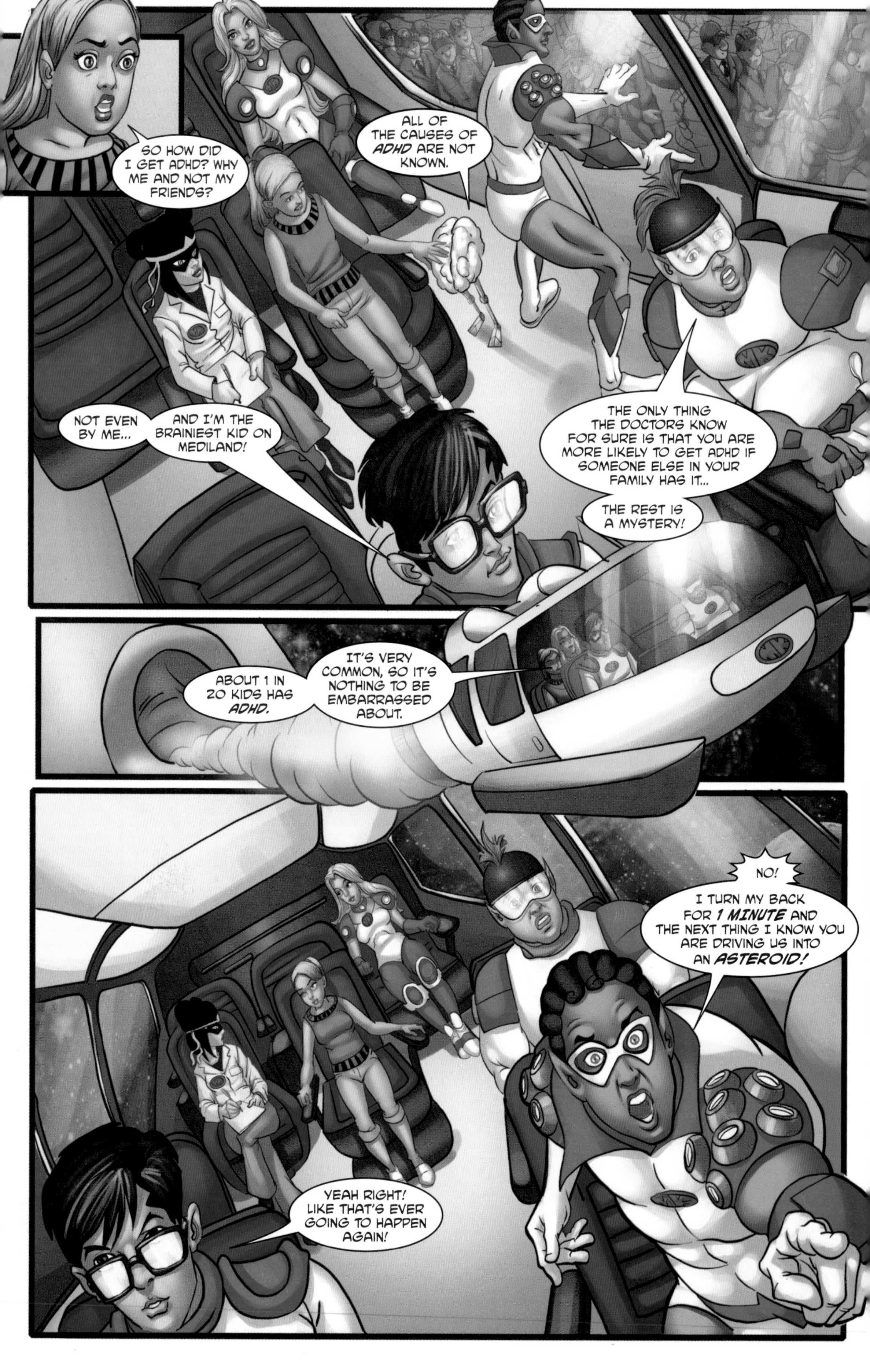
SO HOW DID I GET ADHD? WHY ME AND NOT MY FRIENDS?
ALL OF THE CAUSES OF *ADHD* ARE NOT KNOWN.
NOT EVEN BY ME...
AND I'M THE BRAINIEST KID ON MEDILAND!
THE ONLY THING THE DOCTORS KNOW FOR SURE IS THAT YOU ARE MORE LIKELY TO GET ADHD IF SOMEONE ELSE IN YOUR FAMILY HAS IT...
THE REST IS A MYSTERY!
ABOUT 1 IN 20 KIDS HAS *ADHD.*
IT'S VERY COMMON, SO IT'S NOTHING TO BE EMBARRASSED ABOUT.
NO!
I TURN MY BACK FOR ***1 MINUTE*** AND THE NEXT THING I KNOW YOU ARE DRIVING US INTO AN ***ASTEROID!***
YEAH RIGHT! LIKE THAT'S EVER GOING TO HAPPEN AGAIN!

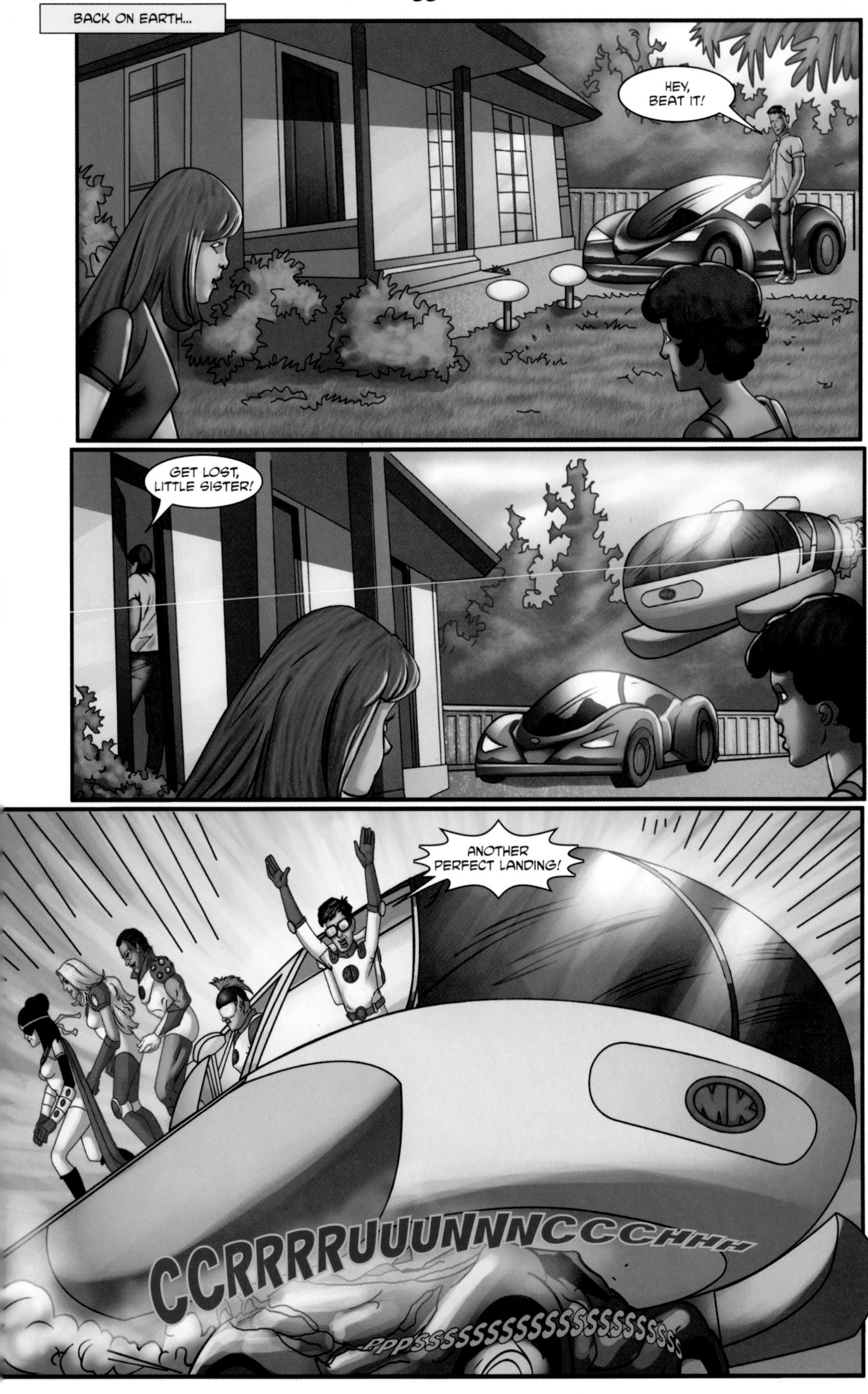
BACK ON EARTH...
HEY, BEAT IT!
GET LOST, LITTLE SISTER!
ANOTHER PERFECT LANDING!
CCRRRRUUUNNNCCCCHHH
PPPSSSSSSSSSSSSSSSSSSSSS

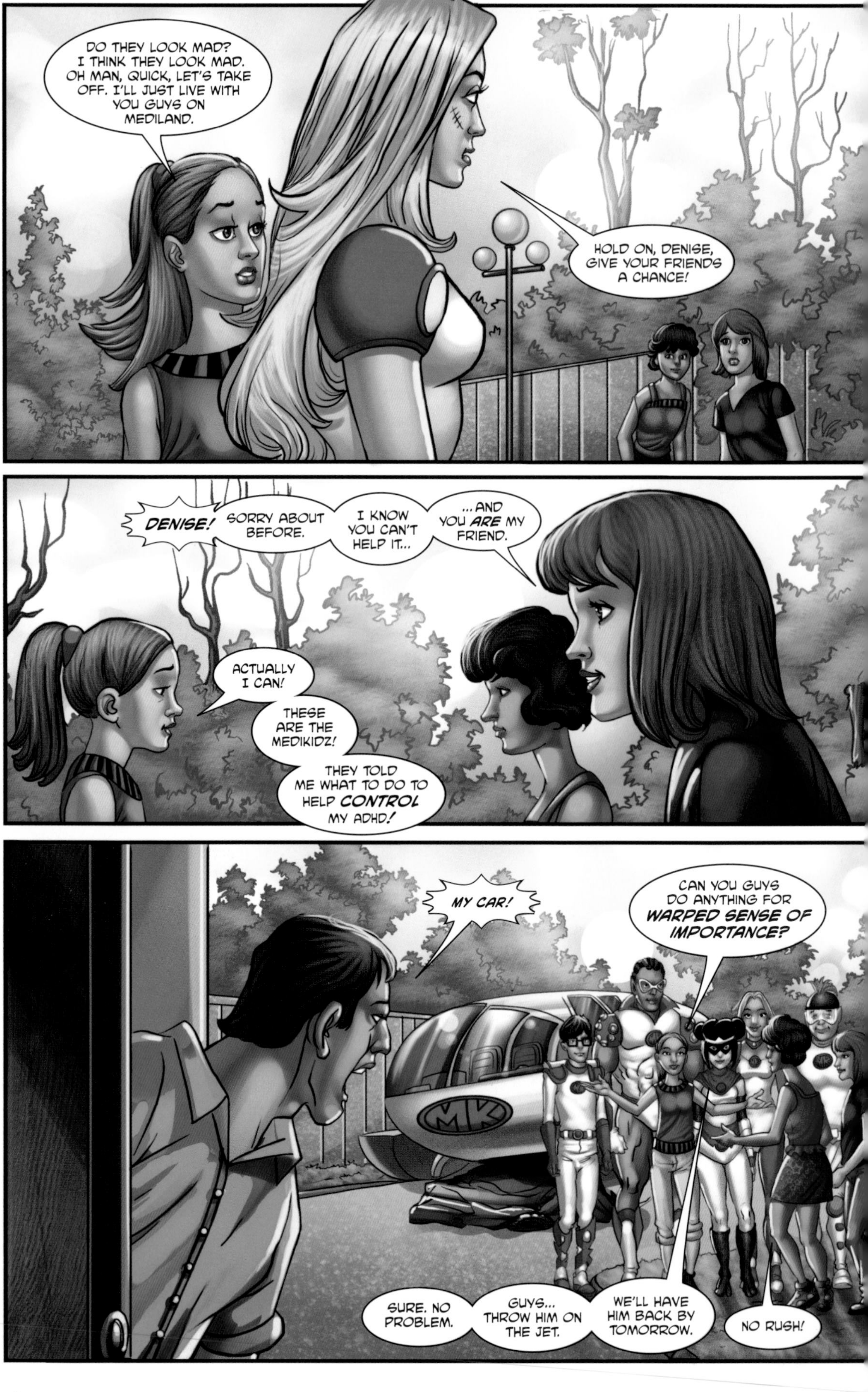
DO THEY LOOK MAD? I THINK THEY LOOK MAD. OH MAN, QUICK, LET'S TAKE OFF. I'LL JUST LIVE WITH YOU GUYS ON MEDILAND.
HOLD ON, DENISE, GIVE YOUR FRIENDS A CHANCE!
DENISE!
SORRY ABOUT BEFORE.
I KNOW YOU CAN'T HELP IT...
...AND YOU ARE MY FRIEND.
ACTUALLY I CAN!
THESE ARE THE MEDIKIDZ!
THEY TOLD ME WHAT TO DO TO HELP CONTROL MY ADHD!
MY CAR!
CAN YOU GUYS DO ANYTHING FOR WARPED SENSE OF IMPORTANCE?
MK
SURE. NO PROBLEM.
GUYS... THROW HIM ON THE JET.
WE'LL HAVE HIM BACK BY TOMORROW.
NO RUSH!

GLOSSARY

ATTENTION DEFICIT HYPERACTIVITY DISORDER (ADHD)
A MILD TO SEVERE MEDICAL DISORDER THAT IS
CHARACTERIZED BY IMPULSIVITY AND OVERACTIVITY,
AND THE INABILITY TO FOCUS, CONCENTRATE, AND PAY
ATTENTION FOR LONG PERIODS OF TIME.

BRAIN THE CENTER OF THE HUMAN NERVOUS SYSTEM. IT
CONTROLS THOUGHT, INVOLUNTARY MOVEMENT IN THE
BODY, BALANCE, GROWTH, AND TEMPERATURE CONTROL.

CEREBRAL HEMISPHERE EITHER OF THE TWO SYMMETRICAL
HALVES OF THE FRONT PART OF THE BRAIN
(CEREBRUM).

CEREBRUM THE FRONT PART OF THE BRAIN, DIVIDED INTO
TWO SYMMETRICAL HALVES (CEREBRAL HEMISPHERES).
IN HUMANS, IT IS WHERE ACTIVITIES SUCH AS
REASONING, LEARNING, SENSORY PERCEPTION, AND
EMOTIONAL RESPONSES TAKE PLACE.

DOPAMINE A CHEMICAL COMPOUND THAT OCCURS IN THE
BRAIN; A NEURUOTRANSMITTER.

FOCUS TO CONCENTRATE EFFORT OR ATTENTION ON A
PARTICULAR THING OR AN ASPECT OF A THING.

FRONTAL LOBE THE PART OF THE BRAIN THAT IS LOCATED
AT THE FRONT OF EACH CEREBRAL HEMISPHERE. IT
IS ASSOCIATED WITH REASONING, PLANNING, PARTS
OF SPEECH AND MOVEMENT, EMOTIONS, AND PROBLEM-
SOLVING.

HYPERACTIVITY EXCESSIVELY ACTIVE, RESTLESS,
AND IMPULSIVE BEHAVIOR; LACKING THE ABILITY TO
CONCENTRATE FOR ANY LENGTH OF TIME, ESPECIALLY
AS A RESULT OF ATTENTION DEFICIT DISORDER.

IMPULSIVE ACTING OR SPEAKING WITHOUT THINKING OR
CONSIDERING CONSEQUENCES; HAVING A TENDENCY
TO ACT ON SUDDEN URGES OR DESIRES.

INATTENTION INABILITY TO PAY ATTENTION; FAILURE
TO TAKE PROPER CARE OR GIVE ENOUGH ATTENTION
TO SOMETHING.

LOBES ROUNDED DIVISIONS OR PROJECTIONS OF
ORGANS OR PARTS IN THE BODY, ESPECIALLY IN THE
LUNGS, BRAIN, OR LIVER.

MRI SCAN MAGNETIC RESONANCE IMAGING TECHNIQUE
    THAT USES ELECTROMAGNETIC RADIATION TO GET
    IMAGES OF THE BODY'S SOFT TISSUES, SUCH AS THE
    BRAIN. THE BODY IS SUBJECTED TO A MAGNETIC
    FIELD, ALLOWING TINY SIGNALS FROM ATOMIC NUCLEI
    TO BE DETECTED AND THEN PROCESSED AND
    CONVERTED INTO IMAGES THAT ARE READ BY A
    COMPUTER.
NEURONS CELLS OF THE NERVOUS SYSTEM THAT ARE
    SPECIALIZED TO CARRY "MESSAGES" TO AND FROM
    THE BRAIN AND TO OTHER PARTS OF THE BODY.
NEUROTRANSMITTERS CHEMICAL SUBSTANCES PRODUCED
    BY THE BODY THAT ACT AS MESSENGERS OR SIGNAL
    CARRIERS.
NORADRENALINE ALSO KNOWN AS NOREPINEPHRINE; A
    HORMONE AND NEUROTRANSMITTER, SECRETED BY
    THE ADRENAL GLAND. IT INCREASES BLOOD PRESSURE
    AND RATE AND DEPTH OF BREATHING, RAISES THE
    LEVEL OF BLOOD SUGAR, AND DECREASES THE
    ACTIVITY OF THE INTESTINES.
OCCIPITAL LOBE THE PYRAMID-SHAPED PART OF THE BRAIN
    THAT IS LOCATED AT THE BACK OF EACH HEMISPHERE.
    IT ACTS AS THE VISUAL PROCESSING CENTER OF THE
    BRAIN.
PARIETAL LOBE THE PART OF THE BRAIN THAT IS LOCATED
    ABOVE THE OCCIPITAL LOBE AND BEHIND THE FRONTAL
    LOBE. IT IS CONCERNED WITH STIMULI RELATED TO
    TOUCH, PRESSURE, TEMPERATURE, AND PAIN.
SHIFT A CHANGE OF ONE SET OF WORKERS FOR ANOTHER;
    A SCHEDULED PERIOD OF WORK OR DUTY, AS IN NIGHT
    SHIFT.
SIDE EFFECT AN UNDESIRABLE SECONDARY EFFECT OF A
    DRUG OR OTHER FORM OF MEDICAL TREATMENT.
SPLEEN A DUCTLESS ORGAN IN THE LEFT UPPER ABDOMEN
    OF PEOPLE AND OTHER VERTEBRATES THAT HELPS TO
    DESTROY OLD RED BLOOD CELLS, FORM WHITE BLOOD
    CELLS, AND STORE BLOOD.
TEMPORAL LOBE THE PART OF THE BRAIN THAT IS LOCATED
    ON BOTH THE RIGHT AND LEFT SIDES. IT IS
    CONCERNED WITH HEARING AND MEMORY.

FOR MORE INFORMATION

ADD WAREHOUSE (CATALOG AND SUPPLIES)
300 NORTHWEST SEVENTIETH AVENUE, SUITE 102
PLANTATION, FL 33317
(800) 233-9273
WEB SITE: HTTP://ADDWAREHOUSE.COM
ADD WAREHOUSE PROVIDES A VARIETY OF DIFFERENT
        EDUCATIONAL AND TRAINING BOOKS, VIDEOS, AND
        OTHER MATERIALS ON ATTENTION DEFICIT DISORDER
        (ADD) AND ADHD FOR TEENS AND PARENTS.

CENTRE FOR ADD/ADHD ADVOCACY, CANADA
40 WYNFORD DRIVE
SUITE 304B
TORONTO, ON M3C 1J5
CANADA
(416) 637-8584
WEB SITE: HTTP://WWW.CADDAC.CA
THIS ORGANIZATION PROVIDES LEADERSHIP IN ADHD
        EDUCATION AND ADVOCACY FOR PEOPLE ACROSS
        CANADA.

CENTERS FOR DISEASE CONTROL AND PREVENTION
1600 CLIFTON ROAD
ATLANTA, GA 30333
WEB SITE: HTTP://WWW.CDC.COM
THIS AGENCY IS A PART OF THE U.S. DEPARTMENT OF HEALTH
        AND HUMAN SERVICES. IT PROMOTES GOOD HEALTH
        AND PREVENTION OF DISEASES AND IT WORKS TO
        DEVELOP PUBLIC HEALTH POLICIES AND TO ENCOURAGE
        HEALTHY BEHAVIORS.

CHILDREN AND ADULTS WITH ATTENTION DEFICIT DISORDER
(CHAAD)
8181 PROFESSIONAL PLACE, SUITE 150
LANDOVER, MD 20785
(800) 233-4050
WEB SITE: HTTP://WWW.CHADD.ORG
WITH MORE THAN 20,000 MEMBERS, CHADD IS ONE OF
        THE LARGEST NONPROFIT ORGANIZATIONS DEDICATED
        TO SERVING THE NEEDS OF CHILDREN, TEENS, AND
        ADULTS WITH ADD AND ADHD.

HEALTH CANADA
ADDRESS LOCATOR 0900C2
OTTAWA, ON K1A OK9
CANADA
(866) 225-0709

WEB SITE: HTTP://WWW.HC-SC.GC.CA
THIS CANADIAN ORGANIZATION WORKS TO HELP CANADIANS
MAINTAIN AND IMPROVE THEIR HEALTH AND PROVIDES
INFORMATION ABOUT HEALTH-RELATED TOPICS.

MAYO CLINIC
WEB SITE: HTTP://WWW.MAYOCLINIC.COM
MAYO CLINIC IS A NOT-FOR-PROFIT PRACTICE THAT WORKS
TO HELP PROVIDE INFORMATION TO THE PUBLIC AND
HEALTH PROFESSIONALS ABOUT VARIOUS ILLNESSES,
CONDITIONS, AND MEDICAL RESEARCH. IT PROVIDES
SERVICES IN ROCHESTER, MINNESOTA, JACKSONVILLE,
FLORIDA, AND PHOENIX AND SCOTTSDALE, ARIZONA.

SAMHSA'S NATIONAL MENTAL HEALTH INFORMATION CENTER
P.O. BOX 2345
ROCKVILLE, MD 20847
(800) 789-2647
WEB SITE: HTTP://MENTALHEALTH.SAMHSA.GOV
THIS CENTER FOR MENTAL HEALTH SERVICES PROVIDES
INFORMATION ABOUT MENTAL HEALTH FOR YOUNG
PEOPLE AND SERVICES FOR INDIVIDUALS, FAMILIES,
THE GENERAL PUBLIC, AND HEALTH PROVIDERS.

U.S. NATIONAL LIBRARY OF MEDICINE
NATIONAL INTITUTES OF HEALTH
U.S. HEALTH AND HUMAN SERVICES
8600 ROCKVILLE PIKE
BETHESDA, MD 20894
(888) 346-3656
WEB SITE: HTTP://WWW.NLM.NIH.GOV
THE NATIONAL LIBRARY OF MEDICINE PROVIDES
INFORMATION ABOUT SCIENCE AND HEALTH, INCLUDING
DATA ABOUT ADHD, TO THE PUBLIC, SCIENTISTS, AND
HEALTH PROFESSIONALS.

WEB SITES

DUE TO THE CHANGING NATURE OF INTERNET LINKS, ROSEN
PUBLISHING HAS DEVELOPED AN ONLINE LIST OF WEB SITES
RELATED TO THE SUBJECT OF THIS BOOK. THIS SITE IS UPDATED
REGULARLY. PLEASE USE THIS LINK TO ACCESS THE LIST:

HTTP://WWW.ROSENLINKS.COM/MED/ADHD

ALLOSSO, DAN. *OUTSIDE THE BOX*. LINCOLN, NE: IUNIVERSE, 2007.

BRINKERHOFF, SHIRLEY. *STUCK ON FAST FORWARD: YOUTH WITH ATTENTION-DEFICIT/HYPERACTIVITY DISORDER (YOUTH WITH SPECIAL NEEDS)*. BROOMALL, PA: MASON CREST PUBLISHERS, 2007.

FOX, JANET S. *GET ORGANIZED WITHOUT LOSING IT*. MINNEAPOLIS, MN: FREE SPIRIT PUBLISHING, 2006.

HALLOWELL, EDWARD M., AND JOHN J. RATEY. *DELIVERED FROM DISTRACTION: GETTING THE MOST OUT OF LIFE WITH ATTENTION DEFICIT DISORDER*. NEW YORK, NY: BALLANTINE BOOKS, 2006.

MOSS, SAMANTHA, AND LESLEY SCHWARTZ. *WHERE'S MY STUFF? THE ULTIMATE TEEN ORGANIZING GUIDE*. SAN FRANCISCO, CA: ZEST BOOKS, 2007.

NADEAU, KATHLEEN G., AND ELLEN B. DIXON. *LEARNING TO SLOW DOWN AND PAY ATTENTION: A BOOK FOR KIDS ABOUT ADHD*. 3RD ED. WASHINGTON, DC: MAGINATION PRESS, 2004.

PETERSEN, CHRISTINE. *DOES EVERYONE HAVE ADHD? A TEEN'S GUIDE TO DIAGNOSIS AND TREATMENT*. NEW YORK, NY: CHILDREN'S PRESS, 2007.

POMERE, JONAS. *FREQUENTLY ASKED QUESTIONS ABOUT ADD AND ADHD (FAQ: TEEN LIFE)*. NEW YORK, NY: ROSEN PUBLISHING GROUP, INC., 2007.

QUINN, PATRICIA O., AND JUDITH M. STERN. *PUTTING ON THE BRAKES: UNDERSTANDING AND TAKING CONTROL OF YOUR ADD OR ADHD*. WASHINGTON, DC: MAGINATION PRESS, 2008.

STEER, JOANNE, AND KATE HORSTMANN. *HELPING KIDS AND TEENS WITH ADHD IN SCHOOL: A WORKBOOK FOR CLASSROOM SUPPORT AND MANAGING TRANSITIONS*. PHILADELPHIA, PA: JESSICA KINGSLEY PUBLISHERS, 2009.

STRONG, JEFF, MICHAEL O. FLANAGAN, AND LITO TAJEDA-FLORES. *ADD/ADHD FOR DUMMIES*. HOBOKEN, NJ: WILEY PUBLISHING, 2005.

TAYLOR, BLAKE E. S. ADHD AND ME: *WHAT I LEARNED FROM LIGHTING FIRES AT THE DINNER TABLE*. OAKLAND, CA: NEW HARBINGER PUBLICATIONS, 2007.

TAYLOR, JOHN F. *THE SURVIVAL GUIDE FOR KIDS WITH ADD OR ADHD*. MINNEAPOLIS, MN: FREE SPIRIT PUBLISHING, 2006.

WALKER, JOYCE. *AD/HD TEENS: DISTRACTED OR DEFIANT? COACHING HELPS! COACHING STRATEGIES FOR ADOLESCENTS, PARENTS, TEACHERS, AND COACHES*. LINCOLN, NE: IUNIVERSE, 2006.

ZEIGLER DENDY, CHRIS A., AND ALEX ZEIGLER. *A BIRD'S EYE VIEW OF LIFE WITH ADD AND ADHD: ADVICE FROM YOUNG SURVIVORS*. 2ND ED. CEDAR BLUFF, AL: CHERISH THE CHILDREN, 2007.

A
ATTENTION SPAN, 22

B
BRAIN, 8, 10-21, 22, 24, 25,
        26-27

C
CAUSES, 32

D
DIAGNOSES, 24
DOPAMINE, 19, 20, 25

E
EXECUTIVE FUNCTIONING, 16

F
FOCUS, 16, 25
FRONTAL LOBE, 14, 15, 16, 21,
        22, 24, 25, 26
FUNCTIONAL MRI SCAN, 24

H
HARMONY, 27
HYPERACTIVITY, 23

I
IMPULSIVENESS, 23
INATTENTION, 23

M
MEDICINE, 25, 28, 29, 30

N
NEURONS, 8, 17-21, 22, 27
NEUROTRANSMITTERS, 18-21,
        22, 25-27
NORADRENALINE, 19, 20, 25

O
OCCIPITAL LOBE, 13, 16, 21

P
PARIETAL LOBE, 12, 16
PATIENCE, 30
PSYCHIATRITSTS, 30
PSYCHOLOGISTS, 30

S
SIDE EFFECTS, 28
SYMPTOMS, 22, 23, 29

T
TEMPORAL LOBE, 13, 14, 16, 21
THERAPISTS, 30
THERAPY, 30, 31
TREATMENT, 25, 28, 29, 30-31

ABOUT THE AUTHORS

DR. KIM CHILMAN-BLAIR IS A MEDICAL DOCTOR WITH TEN YEARS OF EXPERIENCE IN MEDICAL WRITING AND A PASSION FOR PROVIDING MEDICAL INFORMATION THAT MAKES CHILDREN WANT TO LEARN.

JOHN TADDEO, FORMALLY OF MARVEL ENTERTAINMENT, IS A CELEBRATED COMIC BOOK WRITER AND DIRECTOR OF TWO AWARD-WINNING ANIMATED SHORTS.